"The poems in *Resistance: Righteous Rage in the Age of #MeToo* do more than resist: they testify and bear witness, grieve and lament, howl and spark, "disrupt and name the rape culture that has been normalized and inherent in our society," as Sue Goyette writes in her Foreword. Richly textured and exquisitely nuanced, these raw and unflinching poems will break your heart open, stun you with their courage, their depth and hard-earned resilience. A deeply moving and urgently necessary collection." —LISA RICHTER, author or *Closer to Where We Began* and *Nautilus and Bone*

"Sue Goyette's anthology *Resistance* claims poetry is essential to processing pain, Oprah claims being assaulted 'changes you,' and in this way *Resistance* speaks the voices of the changed and gives space to those who now live with shame, brokenness, shattered ideals and perceptions, and a comprehension of diminished safety. When #MeToo hit the internet, I was both shocked and unsurprised at how many hands went up around me, and how many memories came out of the closet like ghosts. Goyette claims this violence is epidemic, and these voices can seek to claim safety back through 'resilience and resistance.'"
—MICHELINE MAYLOR, author of *Little Wildheart* and *The Bad Wife*

"*Resistance* is a monument to defiance against a terrible, pervasive darkness, demanding our attention and action. As readers we bear witness, but the anger that is sparked at the magnitude of the injustice of sexual assault is profound; I hope we are driven to dismantle and rebuild the systems that fail us, and work towards restitution for those of us still carrying ourselves forward with our stories, every day."
—NISHA PATEL, author of *Limited Success* and *Coconut*

"Seventy-eight soul-shattering voices that refuse to be silenced or ashamed. *Resistance* provides the megaphone." —JENNIFER MUSIAL, Assistant Professor, Department of Women's and Gender Studies, New Jersey City University

"This volume of poetry represents the sexual assault equivalent of the residential school inquiry transcripts and begs for another truth and reconciliation commission. Surely the recommendations arising from that scrutiny would help to guide all aspects of the justice system when trying these all-too-common cases. Injustice concerning sexual assault cannot be underestimated: *Resistance* should be required reading for all Canadian legislators." —PATRICIA FELL, Artistic Director, Windsor Feminist Theatre

RESISTANCE
RIGHTEOUS RAGE IN THE AGE OF #METOO

EDITED BY SUE GOYETTE

University of Regina Press

Copyright © 2021 University of Regina Press.

All rights reserved. No part of this work covered by the copyrights hereon may be reproduced or used in any form or by any means—graphic, electronic, or mechanical—without the prior written permission of the publisher. Any request for photocopying, recording, taping or placement in information storage and retrieval systems of any sort shall be directed in writing to Access Copyright.

Printed and bound in Canada at Imprimerie Gauvin. The text of this book is printed on 100% post-consumer recycled paper with earth-friendly vegetable-based inks.

COVER AND TEXT DESIGN: Duncan Noel Campbell
COPY EDITOR: Kelly Laycock
PROOFREADER: Donna Grant
COVER IMAGE: "Ophelia," by Renée Munn.

Library and Archives Canada Cataloguing in Publication

TITLE: Resistance : righteous rage in the age of #MeToo / edited by Sue Goyette.

OTHER TITLES: Righteous rage in the age of #MeToo | Righteous rage in the age of hashtag me too

NAMES: Goyette, Sue, 1964- editor.

IDENTIFIERS: Canadiana (print) 20210106441 | Canadiana (ebook) 2021010841X | ISBN 9780889778016 (softcover) | ISBN 9780889778078 (hardcover) | ISBN 9780889778030 (PDF) | ISBN 9780889778054 (EPUB)

SUBJECTS: LCSH: Women—Crimes against—Poetry. | LCSH: Women—Violence against—Poetry. | LCSH: Sexual abuse victims—Poetry. | LCSH: Rape victims—Poetry. | LCSH: Sex crimes—Poetry. | LCSH: Women—Poetry. | LCSH: Women—Social conditions—Poetry. | LCSH: MeToo movement—Poetry. | CSH: Canadian poetry (English)—21st century. | LCGFT: Poetry.

CLASSIFICATION: LCC PS8287.S49 R47 2021 | DDC C811/.60803526949—dc23

University of Regina Press

University of Regina Press, University of Regina, Regina, Saskatchewan, Canada, S4S 0A2
TEL: (306) 585-4758 FAX: (306) 585-4699
WEB: www.uofrpress.ca

10 9 8 7 6 5 4 3 2 1

We acknowledge the support of the Canada Council for the Arts for our publishing program. We acknowledge the financial support of the Government of Canada. / Nous reconnaissons l'appui financier du gouvernement du Canada. This publication was made possible with support from Creative Saskatchewan's Book Publishing Production Grant Program.

To the families of the Missing and Murdered Indigenous Women and Girls and 2SLGBTQQIA *people. To the voices we aren't hearing. And to those who are learning to listen.*

This poetry anthology deals with sexual assault and abuse in its many forms and may be disturbing to some readers.

CONTENTS

Foreword — *Sue Goyette* xiii

INNOCENCE / EXPOSURE

the telling — *Natalie Baker* 3
No Emergency — *Tara Borin* 4
little monster — *Linda M. Crate* 5
Zipper — *Catherine Graham* 6
Arcadia — *gillian harding-russell* 7
For Lovetta, With Sorrow — *Laurie Mackie* 9
Black Plums — *Catherine Greenwood* 11
In the Scheme of Things — *Raye Hendrickson* 13
Falling Off a Ladder — *Louisa Howerow* 14
Driving Test — *Anne Lévesque* 15
649 Sun Row — *Kelly Nickie* 16
Memory, re-sequenced — *Kim Mannix* 18
Lessons in Womanhood — *Dana Morenstein* 19
Girls Shouldn't — *Yanick Cadieux* 21
Sun, Moon and Thalia — *Kristie Betts Letter* 23
She Looks for Lions — *Bev Brenna* 24
Sixteen — *Eleonore Schönmaier* 25
Teenager Robbed — *Danielle Wong* 27
The Rape of Leda — *Joan Crate* 29
Normalized — *Jesse Holth* 31
Try Me — *Jo Jefferson* 39
Six Minutes of Spring — *Shannon Kernaghan* 40
The Elephant — *Marion Mutala* 41

ENDURANCE / PERSISTENCE

Night Class — *Taryn Hubbard* 45
a death so close — *Rosemary Anderson* 46
The Next Day — *Suzanne Wood* 48
A Victim — *Carol Alexander* 49

Brain Washing — *Ronnie R. Brown* 50
I don't like to tell people I was raped — *Elizabeth Johnston* 51
The Morning After — *Samantha Fitzpatrick* 52
Birdman — *Byrna Barclay* 54
Chance Encounter in the Uranium City Hotel — *Marion Beck* 56
I Ache — *Maroula Blades* 57
A Metaphor — *Jill M. Talbot* 58
Solitary — *Marina Nemat* 59
Pulp Non-fiction — *Janis Butler Holm* 60
Woods Wolf Girl — *Cornelia Hoogland* 61
P.O.ed — *Halli Lilburn* 62
A good thing to know — *Myrna Garanis* 63
"What we did not know in 1972. What has changed." — *Penn Kemp* ... 64
Honour Killing: A Glosa — *Troni Y. Grande* 69

RAGE / RESISTANCE

An Army of Staring Women — *Susie Berg* 73
Fuck Ghomeshi — *Lori Hanson* 74
Five Parts Rape Poem One Part Self-Care — *Kyla Jamieson* 76
The power in a name — *Heather Read* 79
A consideration of the bus driver — *dee Hobsbawn-Smith* 82
The Maid and the Wolf — *Ashley-Elizabeth Best* 83
The Rape of Lucia — *Keith Inman* 84
Pinned, Mounted — *Amber Moore* 85
Chrysalis — *Lucie Kavanagh* 86
Claiming My Brother's Body — *Keir* 88
LXVIII — *Sonnet L'Abbé* 89
When you looked at me did you see me? — *Ellie Rose Langston* 90
abuse victim — *Marianne Jones* 92
Not even trees should grow there — *Emma Lee* 93
The No Variations — *Katherine Lawrence* 94
Name Me After a Fish — *Leah MacLean-Evans* 95
The Way the Crocodile Taught Me — *Katrina Naomi* 96
Molly — *Polly Johnson* 97
Not Guilty — *Donna J.A. Olson* 99
Autumn in the East, the Pilot — *Jami Macarty* 100
The Man Who Studied Love — *Bruce Rice* 101

FOREWORD

Sue Goyette

The anthology you are holding was first inspired by the events leading up to and surrounding the sexual assault trial of Canadian musician and broadcaster Jian Ghomeshi in early 2016. The Ghomeshi case seemed to instigate a breach in what had been a collective and public silence. Women began talking—out loud, on social media, and to each other—in a way I hadn't heard before. Eventually, this coalesced as a movement on social media under the hashtag MeToo, as more and more women came forward with accusations of sexual assault by high-profile men in Hollywood, in the media, and across many professions.

In my community, too, women were talking. I organized a gathering for whoever needed the comfort of company. Some in attendance spoke of their own experiences of sexual assault. Others chose to listen. The air in the room thrummed. The trauma, violence, and wounds of those experiences were exported from silence and individual bodies into a space that held the pain collectively. The relief of hefting that weight off of ourselves was palpable. And this hefting was no small thing.

Around this time, I was approached about editing an anthology of poems that would serve as an extension to that kind of space—a space, here on the page, that would invite readers into this relief from silence. Each poet who answered the call to be part of this anthology is contributing to the change that the #MeToo movement continues to inspire. Unfortunately, there were unexpected challenges when it came time to publish the collection. At each juncture, I contacted contributors to hear how they wanted to proceed: every time, they chose to continue. I am so grateful for each of these poets, for their courage and for their fortitude. Their strength and conviction is what persists and what is so crucial. Waiting in the liminal space between private and public with our writing is challenging. Being in that liminal space considering the theme of this anthology is singular and active and something I've been keenly aware of. Holding this space has become one of the most important roles I've sustained as the editor of this collection.

But now, here we are at last: at the point of publication. Like many crucial journeys, this one seems to have taken us back to where we began, yet changed somehow. I began writing this foreword five years ago, but the words resonate with the same urgency today. The injustice that sparked the #MeToo movement remains an ongoing challenge we face and endure in the systemic, patriarchal, white-bodied, late-capitalist times we find ourselves in. And in the midst of this global pandemic, the climate crisis, and overt and violent racist and oppressive events, may your vitality activate and embody the change we need for a more equitable and inclusive way of being.

* * *

I've been thinking of writing this foreword for months. I knew I wanted to say how important I think this book is. How the #MeToo movement has instigated meaningful conversations about sexual assault, violence, and trauma. I wanted to tell you that what you're holding in your hands is a collective of people who have chosen poetry to process an experience of violence. How this reclamation of voice is crucial for the way it disrupts and names the rape culture that has become normalized and inherent in our society and how making art can help process experiences of violence and trauma. I wanted to reiterate how poetry is essential for some of us in how we process our pain. I'd describe it as a form of courage or survival. Resistance. Between thinking of what I wanted to write here and the actual writing, a person close to me was raped and I was reminded, in such proximity, of how deeply traumatizing that violence is. How the experience obliterates self-confidence and vitality while it fertilizes and emblazons shame. Trust, the sustainable and crucial element that binds us, is broken. We feel singular and alone. Unworthy. And unsure. And these feelings are just the beginning.

I was reminded that, while there is excellent support for people who have endured sexual violence, with many good people making sure that the proper care and resources are in place for those in need, those resources and centres are in dire need of more funding, funding that is sustained and that matches the growing need for the support they offer. I was also reminded of how infrequently, if ever, there is a sense of responsibility or accountability from the perpetrator who is raping/assaulting. Without any sense of responsibility or restitution, there is no chance for resolution. When I started writing this, one of the news stories was about a Halifax man who was given a three-year suspended sentence for break and enter and assault charges for breaking into his former girlfriend's apartment after following her home from a bar when she left with someone. The charges for sexual assault and uttering death threats had been dropped after he pleaded guilty. The Crown had been asking for a two-year prison term, followed by two years' probation. The lawyer for the accused claimed that any prison term *would cost his client his future* as he was enrolled to start law school in Ottawa beginning the next month. This is a common occurrence in sexual assault cases. Unbelievably, the well-being of the person who raped or assaulted is given precedence over the person harmed. The person who endured these particular crimes, in her victim statement, said *she dropped out of university as a result of the incident and suffered from panic attacks and flashbacks* sitting in the courtroom and having to endure listening to the judge tell her assailant *that he had a glowing future ahead of him.* The attention and care given to the accused is enraging and happens all too frequently.

This experience of systemic violence combined with the original violence survivors endure provides insight into why many refuse to press charges in the first place. I am truly surprised that I don't combust with the anger I so often feel. The rage. Right now, thinking about this again, I am combustible. And though this is a familiar outcome of almost every account of sexual assault (remember the hockey player at Queen's University whose assault sentence was postponed so he *wouldn't miss his internship?* And on it goes, absurdly, tragically, deplorably, in the same systemic, patriarchal direction), I still feel indignant, troubled, incensed. And these are only the stories we hear about. There are so many voices that are silenced, silent, or remain unheard.

* * *

Chronically, we know, our legal system fails in earnest to ensure justice is served by upholding a rape culture that minimizes the victim's experience and retraumatizes the victim while excusing or pardoning the perpetrator's crime. This is a systemic failure which perpetuates a cultural acceptance that sexual violence is permissible, understandable even. In 2014, the YWCA published the breakdown of numbers of sexual assaults reported to the police. The numbers are an assault in themselves: out of 1,000 sexual assaults, 33 are reported, 29 are recorded as a crime (the police decide whether or not a crime took place, which is problematic for its own obvious reasons), 12 have charges laid, 6 are prosecuted, and 3 lead to a conviction. We know that the unlikelihood of getting a conviction is one of the reasons that people don't report their assailants. Why bother? And for some, who would even hear us?

So first I want to write to those of you holding this book who haven't yet chosen (or might not ever choose) to extract this violence into a form that is more public or even just spoken aloud. Some of you have experienced this violence and may be remaining silent knowing the futility of pressing charges. Some of you may be remaining silent as a righteous protest, not wanting to give the experience any more of yourself than you have to. It doesn't get your voice, and it doesn't get your name. Some of you may be choosing to be silent because the experience defies articulation. It was so unexpected, so painful, that to describe it renews a deep sense of shame and awakens the pain. To describe it is to confirm that the experience actually happened, and that admission would require an adjustment to the idea you hold of yourself. Some of you may be silent because your silence is protecting you and is keeping you safe. Some of you may be silent because you don't trust your voice anymore or are afraid that if you hear yourself say it, you won't be able to stop the undoing of yourself. Some of you feel you have no choice because you believe your voice will not be heard or acknowledged.

Silence *is* a choice. And each of us has our own singular reasons for keeping silence or speaking out, and these reasons are valid and honourable. If and when you do decide to speak, I trust you to know who to break your silence with, and when. There is a list of resources and assault centres at the back of the book. If you're reading this and relating to any of these silences, I hope the weight you bear lightens. I hope that you find this company fortifying. And if it's shame holding your tongue hostage, if it's the thought of what people will think of you, how they may blame you for not making the right choice, for somehow failing to keep yourself safe, I hope this collection reminds you that you are not to blame. I hope you know that you are not alone and that you have done nothing wrong. The problem isn't you. And what you're holding in your hands is the righteous company of people who believe you and believe in you.

Sexual violence isn't about sex: it's about power. And the problem is the hegemonic, patriarchal system that continues to objectify our bodies and dismiss the violence done to our bodies while it supports and condones the behavior and authority of the people perpetuating the assaults. In other words, the problem is how some people are treated. The problem is a system that retraumatizes victims while conceding to the patriarchal power that objectifies and commodifies vulnerable people. We're living in a rape culture that is so complete, so steeped in our day-to-day lives, we are barely aware of it unless we're on the lookout for it, and then, well, we can see it everywhere. According to the Canadian Women's Foundation, sexual assault is the only violent crime in Canada that is not declining.[1] In 2009, dealing with sexual assault and related offences cost the economy an estimated $4.8 billion according to the Department of Justice Canada.[2]

These numbers are more than upsetting for me, as they must be for you. And I wonder how the chronic hyper-vigilance to ward off the inevitability of assault has affected our bodies and spirit. Our verve. How much of our energy has this pre-emptive vigilance cost? I recognize that I'm speaking with the privilege of a white woman, and I want to acknowledge the need for intersectionality in this conversation.

---

1   https://canadianwomen.org/the-facts/sexual-assault-harassment/
2   https://www.justice.gc.ca/eng/rp-pr/cj-jp/victim/rr14_01/p10.html

The impact this reality of violence is having on BIPOC women, children, and 2SLGBTQQIA people is deplorable, dishonourable, and needs to be addressed relentlessly.

The victim is most often placed at the centre of the statistics and the way we address abuse. The onus is on us, the recipients of the violence—not to drink too much, not to leave our drinks untended at a party or in a bar, not to dress too provocatively, not to walk alone at night, not to embody our bodies somehow. We expend a great deal of our energy being resilient. What would change if the time spent informing women and children how to avoid sexual assault was spent instead on rehabilitating and educating the people who are raping and assaulting? The focus on pre-emptive action or avoidance misses the actual problem: that sexual violence happens in the first place and that it continues to be a permissible epidemic of violence, and in the case of Indigenous women and girls, a femicide. Where are the assailants and *their* accountability in this conversation? How can we consider and work with the normalized understanding that their actions are beyond the law (not to mention basic human respect and equity), so that responsibility, reparation, and resolution can occur for everyone involved? These are my big questions. If only three out of a 1,000 perpetrators are convicted, where are the rest of the perpetrators in that crowded room and what do they have to say to us?

* * *

One of the things that recharges my spirit is reading about the activism that is becoming more vocal and more frequent. Emily Sulkowicz, the Columbia University student who carried around her 50-pound mattress in an endurance art performance entitled *Mattress Performance (Carry that Weight)* as her senior thesis for her arts degree, generated some necessary conversation in 2014–15. She said the piece would end when the student she alleges raped her in her dorm room was expelled. There is also a growing movement of online resilience including sites like *Hollaback!* (ihollaback.org), which offers support and community-building opportunities. And *Sexual Assault: The Roadshow* is a pop-up, participatory billboard, gallery, and workshop housed in a shipping container that is doing the righteous work of exploring how art can educate us about sexual violence in Ontario. Artistic director Lillian Allen is quoted in a *Now Toronto* article as saying: "We like to think about ways people can resist and things people can do to feel a sense of empowerment and to empower each other. We like turning points. We want people to connect with that kind of agency and to help amplify that."[3] This kind of thinking redeems me. These websites have lists of other forms of activism being done globally that are also worth checking out. This is the way we are keeping each other informed and connected: online and rhizomely.

Another example of activism and art is the commemorative art installation *Walking With Our Sisters,* a memorial that honours missing and murdered Indigenous women, girls, Two-Spirit people, and their families. The impact of the loss is reflected in more than 1,800 pairs of moccasin tops (vamps) made by contributing artists "that were left unfinished for the over 1,180 sisters, mothers, aunties, daughters, cousins, grandmothers, wives, and partners whose lives were tragically cut short over the last thirty years."[4] Over 100 pairs of children's vamps were also included, representing the children who did not return home from residential schools. The memorial had its closing ceremony in August 2019. Also of significance in 2019 was that the National Inquiry into Missing and Murdered Indigenous Women and Girls presented its Final Report to families, survivors, Indigenous leaders, as well as to federal and provincial governments. I urge you all to read the report, which is available online.[5] There are so many voices missing from this conversation and so many voices yet to be honoured.

These are only a few examples of empowerment and of what personal care and resolution look like. Thankfully, we are seeing more of this spirit, but now I want the paradigm to shift, now I want the attention to be on the people raping and assaulting. Now I want accountability and justice. And while I'm at it, I want the kind of judicial and policy changes that end systemic violence. And I want way more money poured into trauma-informed support for people enduring the violence and its ongoing impact.

---

3   https://nowtoronto.com/sexual-assault-the-road-show-is-about-resistance-and-empowerment
4   http://walkingwithoursisters.ca/
5   https://www.mmiwg-ffada.ca/final-report/

In the meantime, I offer this collection, which will be at home in the company of the activism that is continuing to erupt in communities and on social media as well as at home with the people who need it privately. Each person's response in this anthology is as singular as they are and yet what they have in common is their refusal for anyone else's version to occupy their first person. Here, then, is a righteous collection of "I"s standing together. As I've said, I've been thinking about writing this foreword for months. I knew I wanted to say how important I think this book is. And it is.

I am a childhood trauma survivor. And I was fourteen when a boyfriend raped me. In the days and years after, my voice found a pen and some paper, and I wrote until I could feel myself again. This took time, but extracting the experience from my body onto paper was an elemental part of the work I did to heal. I am so grateful to have been able to curate a space for these voices and for their poems to do their own essential and fortifying work. Reading through the large pile of submissions, it became clear to me how each voice is a crucial reclamation of power. These are the voices you're about to read.

I urge you to share this work with whoever needs their company. This is what change looks like. All of us, contributing in whatever way we can: by writing and by reading, by sharing and by listening to the experiences we have in common. May this collection of poems give you courage. May it help to continue the contagion of change that defies violence and injustice. In this way, the numbers are on our side. We are a multitude, resilient and resisting. And, once our experiences have been dignified by our voices, however that sounds or looks, once we feel the lightness and the relief of having borne and then disrupted our pain, there is no telling what else we can do.

Sue Goyette
K'jipuktuk (Halifax)
the ancestral, unceded, and unsurrendered territory
of the Mi'kmaq

and i told you no
—LINDA M. CRATE

INNOCENCE / EXPOSURE

THE TELLING
Natalie Baker

i used to say
what i let happen
instead of
what he did
and *i didn't say no*
instead of
i didn't consent

i never knew
there was a
difference

NO EMERGENCY
Tara Borin

Such a small thing,
a body's gesture
between sheets,
one of us ready the other
not
and whose need is more
urgent.

As you storm
my silence
I picture you,

a little boy
who snatched up a garter snake
as it slid into spring sunshine,
tongue gathering your excitement
from the air

and your mother
did she hold her discomfort and
the snake's,
like a love note in her clenched hand,
written but
never read?

She reasoned that
a garter snake won't bite,

boys
will be boys.

LITTLE MONSTER
Linda M. Crate

i was twelve,
and i told you no;
didn't stop
you from trying—
i remember
you pulled on my clothes,
but i refused;
so you stripped down to your
underwear
i flew down the stairs
your sister smiled
and said my mother was there
clearly unaware of what happened
upstairs—
i remember you rejected me
broke up with me because i refused
to compromise my values,
but i'm all i have
i cannot lose myself into the talons
of another's dreams
because i have aspirations of my own
won't be someone's pawn in any game
because life isn't some game of chess;
and we were kids,
but that doesn't excuse your behaviour
a monster is never a gentleman
no matter how much he pretends to be.

ZIPPER
Catherine Graham

Spring meant papercut daffodils
taped to classroom walls,
no crosses like at my best friend's school

where April heat prodded our backs
towards the shortcut. Fresh kittens
at her cousin's house, a nest

of soft, when coming up the hill,
pushing his ten-speed—even then I felt the sun
twist round him, the plunge

of my gut—he used his cycle to gate us,
to block our path, watched us slow, stop.
He checked—no one. The hill

shadowed his dark. The fat tongue on his t-shirt
eager for flavour and beneath it, the growing
pink he'd unzipped—no adults to pull

us back except this twist in the blood said—
run! The mud soft-sucking our shoes.
Don't look, don't fall—

She screamed between our broken breath—
you asked, you touched!—she ran
—*disgusting!*—straight into her cousin's house

while I stood chained to the sound
of the lock sliding time forward
and back into place like a zipper.

ARCADIA
gillian harding-russell

The village green with a fountain for birds
and an elm whose trunk was wide
as three children's embrace (haven
for "What Time Is It,
Mr. Wolf?")

later struck by lightning
that split the tree in a forked way.
In this village built for Westinghouse workers
beside a dark woods with wild strawberries in June
springing up on the leafy floor, the factory's long house
sided by the railway tracks on one side
with farmer's field on the other side

much to explore outside our #6 door,
my brother and sister walking home
along the railway tracks from school, brushed
their hands against purple irises and bulrushes
when I was too young to go. Most of my friends
afraid of the woods but I had walked there
with my brother and learned to identify
the white-throated sparrow's four pensive
notes followed by a quavering arpeggio
to which we gave our own words

and knew the spring beauties, virginal white
with a mauve-pink stripe like a nuance
of desire, where to find the violets on the springy turf
under mossy trees, showed my best friend the trillium
three-petalled, more strange than beautiful
we had learned not to pick, when

on the other side of the ravine in the middle
of the woods, the water was knee high among
the marsh marigolds: a man in a black jacket standing there
calling us over. *Bon jour, jeunes filles* . . .

and my friend knew to flee. This stranger
with greased hair in black leather coat picked flowers
with me, and I was afraid to be impolite. I took flowers
from this man—tall as my big brother but not him

when he crouched over to pick a spring beauty
his arms around my shoulders, I leapt out
of his reach, ran with heart beating

deep into the spring-cold marsh wading through the marigolds
not yet in bloom, as he stumbled after me swearing
—swearing identifiable

in any language—pointed black shoes
in the wilderness so out of place I thought—as I ran fast, fast
as I could through the thick of hundred-year-old trees, at last

finding my way down the curved road
that wound down to our house. My mother at the front
door, angry relieved and angry again, and
relieved. My heart still pounding, trying to explain
what I didn't understand. She put me mud-smeared

into the bathtub and washed me clean, but scrubbed
so hard . . . we waited for my father and big brother
to come back from looking for me (my friend had told

her mother, her mother phoning mine . . .), and so
I worried, too, what it might have been that rubbed off
on me from that goat-footed man wearing ballroom shoes.

FOR LOVETTA, WITH SORROW
Laurie Mackie

Hush, baby, hush,
when you climb the stairs
up to grandma's attic

A monster lives up there

I never knew
he collected us
dollies splayed in naked rows

Puppets on your string.

That neighbour child,
me, your niece,
your own

Precious morsels on display

Even now
must revives
the memories

Live on in murky spaces

Cobwebs
in the corners
bound inside dark places

Shamed, untold but not forgotten

I tried once
the system won

So, hush, baby, hush
when you climb the stairs
up to grandma's attic

The monster still lives up there.

BLACK PLUMS
Catherine Greenwood

I'm getting buzzed on rum
I keep hidden from my wife
here in the dim shed.
Outside in the humming heat
the orchard branches sag—
engorged plums, fleshy peaches
round as a small child's bum.
The wasps getting drunk
on burst cherries.

From behind the wall
I hear my niece playing,
she wants to stroke
the soft feathers of the hens.
Nearly four, the girl still
sucks her thumb like a baby.
I call her in from the heat,
let her feel in my trouser pockets
for sweets.

I teach her to say
Little Jack Horner sat in a corner
eating his Christmas pie.
When she's finished her candy
and licked the juice from her chin,
I show her the trick
that always makes them giggle:
I tweak her nose and poke the nub
of my thumb between my fingers, saying
Oh, oh! What's this?
Who's got your nose?
She crows with excitement
and grabs at me with chubby hands.

It's time for her to learn
the rest of the rhyme:
He stuck in his thumb
and pulled out a plum.
Oh, I am all thumbs today.
I fumble around, pull out
the other candy and say
Look. What's this?
It's a treat for you.
Take it. Quick!

Now look what she's done.
I tuck myself away
and wipe off her sticky
fingers and face with a rag.
Before I send her out
I have her repeat
the game's final line
—Oh, what a bad girl am I—
until I'm satisfied
she's learned to play it
dumb.

IN THE SCHEME OF THINGS
Raye Hendrickson

It wasn't so big, just
an uncle trapping me in
the telephone alcove, his paw
on my teenage breast, his
whispers. My silence and feeling
soiled by more than the dirty
mark he left on my
white sweatshirt.

And it was just a drunk cousin
pinning me in the kitchen with
his foul words breathed
into my face: *You'd be pretty if
you lost weight.* My silence,
feeling ugly in spite of my Christmas
party clothes.

It took years before I could love my body, before
I could believe someone would desire me.
A high price, in the scheme.

FALLING OFF A LADDER
Louisa Howerow

smell of menthol,
his "you'll be okay,"
sour dampness of the shirt.
My saviour—that's what
everyone called him—
checked for broken bones,
found nothing, picked me up,
his arms under my body,
his fingers splayed across
my chest. The pinch.
Such a little thing—wasn't it?

DRIVING TEST
Anne Lévesque

Expo 67. The first
IMAX movie. An uncle.
I do not know what
He has against me
But I know
To pull away
I have never told
My mother

Main Street. The itinerant
Optometrist. Translating
For my mother, whose
Eyes are fine and so
Are mine he tells me,
When she's gone
His hand on my thigh
Casual, jolly-like
I say nothing
To my mother

Driving test. I am nervous. For months
My father and I have argued:
I grind the gears slip the clutch, hate
Being judged, found wanting. Halfway
Through the checklist on his clipboard
The examiner parks his hand
Above my knee
It idles there, surreal
Five heartbeats? Four?
He's played this game before
He knows, to the second,
When to fold
He knows
That I will not tell my mother

INNOCENCE / EXPOSURE — 15

649 SUN ROW
Kelly Nickie

Even though I may not
remember the number
every time I drive by
I can locate it
across from that Presbyterian church
where you said you and your friends played Frisbee on the lawn

Like the church
it has a tall steeple
and a wooden front door
but it is not a holy place
Freshly planted peace lilies
can't hide
the night
my confessions
turned into
your monopoly

Those new Pashmina curtains
conceal
red wine stains &
cannabis ashes on hardwood

The tiny attic window looking out your bedroom
where you told me to loosen up a little
after I told you this wasn't a good idea
can't be seen
from the street

One day
this road
will just be
another throughway
to get from
one street
to
another.

MEMORY, RE-SEQUENCED
Kim Mannix

sparks
around the campfire
the shape of his jaw

a wood floor
the wetness
between my legs

two, four, six-pack
of girls prettier
than me

his hands
snapping
kindling

a mother
not mine
here for her daughter

finally dark
at ten
moon shadows

fill me up, pour me out
only the shape inside
has changed

behind us
someone sings
an owl

LESSONS IN WOMANHOOD
Dana Morenstein

I used to feel around in the dark for signs
that I was more than the small space
between my legs.
Pretending I was a vacant, hollow
ghost of a human person,
as I skipped through busy streets, downtown—
nobody could see me but everyone
would stare.
"Hello, pleased to meet you—I am a ghost."
and their eyes would casually avert themselves
from my flesh, becoming more threatening
each time my running shoe hit
the pavement with a thud,
hips swaying stronger with each spring-loaded step.
I used to tell my mother that she was awful
and that I wanted to die (this was before I actually did)
she'd just look at me with a vacant stare;
responding to my cries with only liquid eyeliner
and carbon black mascara.
I should've known then, that to be a child
was much more powerful than to be
a female body
wildly untamed underneath a shroud
of hidden objects: *shhh—don't tell anyone
that you like it.* "Don't dress like a whore
or they'll lose their fascination with you,
real fast!"
(then you'll be left alone, unwed
and a single mother)
unlike mine, (who married a drunk
and stayed
until the kids were halfway grown
and she had found
a proper replacement) who dressed
in dark dresses

and black tights
with pointy
high-heeled booties she wore
every day to her job as a secretary.
Water the garden and plant the potted perennials,
put a decorative pillow on the *chaise longue*,
these are the things you do, don't do anything
that I wouldn't
(and so, of course, I did).

GIRLS SHOULDN'T
Yanick Cadieux

    We walked up the narrow stairs, in the rundown apartment building, girls trailing behind the men.
    I tugged at the too-tight shirt I had on, wishing it covered my belly button.
    I was uncomfortable showing this much skin.
    My girlfriends were blonde, perky and shiny.
    They looked happy with clothes too small and makeup too dark.
    I did not.

    Little girls should not wear too-tight clothes and too much makeup.

    Once inside, I looked around the apartment, uneasy.
    Loud, hard-hitting music made it so I could barely hear people talk.
    It didn't really matter, though, because the men were engaged in two different conversations and neither was English.
    We shouldn't be here.

    Little girls should not wear too-tight clothes and too much makeup, in a room full of grown men.

    I was uncomfortable and a man with very dark skin, very white teeth and a thick accent, handed me a drink.
    I drank it and relaxed.
    The man handed me another one, and I drank it and laughed.
    He handed me another, and I drank it and danced.
    He handed me one more, I drank it and he slid his arm around my shoulder.
    He handed me a last drink.
    He whispered something I did not comprehend through his thick accent and my haze of thirteen-year-old-drunken, running-to-the-toilet, oh-my-God-I'm-going-to-be-sick confusion.

    Little girls wearing too-tight clothes and too much makeup, should not drink too much.

My friends left me there, on the bathroom floor, sick.
They would come back for me the next day, they promised.
I managed to crawl out of the bathroom to the nearest bedroom and fall asleep.
I woke up in a dark room, with a very dark man on top of me, grunting and showing me his very white teeth.
He was inside me.

Little girls wearing too-tight clothes and too much makeup should not have too much to drink and pass out.

SUN, MOON AND THALIA
Kristie Betts Letter

Thalia's sleeping cheek, dotted with milk and sunlight, burned with delicacy. No flax, no spindles, gluten-free. Groceries wiped with soft cloth, no poisons. This skin took offense to the world's jagged corners, and the pills offered softening from moon-press to sun-prick. Soft ebb of pain and memory, each small moment. When sharpness bled through, Thalia moved to basements, she saw the sharpness, the silver, the spindle holding more and liquid for arm instead mouth. The sleep followed, moon pale. The guys next door, the couple with beautiful flatware, found her, cheek to floorboard. Her babies, a sun and a moon, woke Thalia to the lines, the angels, metallic routine of days. From the fog, shapes cleared and princes lay claim. Thalia wishes for mist when they say *lucky*. Fortune favours some even while they sleep.

SHE LOOKS FOR LIONS
Bev Brenna

at the zoo she paws their cages
fingers playing the cold geography of lines;
she stalks them in bowls of animal crackers
ready to catch a movement, a twitch of the tail

it's not that she likes them
the lions that claw her from play
are ruthless   childhood
lying in ribbons at her feet

and yet she draws them
pencil quivering against the heavy page
better to have it happening now
than later

SIXTEEN
Eleonore Schönmaier

midnight after her student-nursing shift
she knocks on her father's
bedroom door as she promised

her best friend is not allowed
out this late
and lies awake in her bed

her father is asleep, his own underground
shift beginning in the early
morning. He doesn't want her

her father knocks on her
bedroom door
and enters

to walk alone through the forest
so silently they move together
through the stillness of birch

the starlight has five
pointed edges as it drapes
her throat

and spruce trees. What does
her father fear for her? Men, wild dogs,
wolves—they meet only their own

but her father's
face cuts the view
in two

thoughts on the narrow rocky
trail. She leaves her clothes
next to the pump house

INNOCENCE / EXPOSURE—25

*she shared this secret
with her friend
knowing it would be kept*

and swims to the other
shore, her father waiting
among the halo-drone of mosquitoes

*for the adults need
to be protected;
in sixth grade*

she backstrokes and drinks
from the pitcher of milk above
her head

*she whispered
for her friend the word as if it was a seed
that would flower a field yellow*

TEENAGER ROBBED
Danielle Wong

He lay in bed
recovering
He lay in bed
dreaming
He lay in bed
dreaming of his future
He lay in bed
and woke up
He lay in bed
fists pummeling his diaphragm
He lay in bed
his clothes torn off
He lay in bed
hands yanking hard on him
He lay in bed
screaming
He lay in bed
begging to stop
He lay in bed
crying
He lay in bed
knowing
He lay in bed
this doesn't happen to boys
He lay in bed
blaming himself
He lay in bed
he shouldn't be so weak
He lay in bed
he should have been able to fight
He lay in bed
he was so stupid
He lay in bed
wondering what he did wrong

He lay in bed
dreaming
He lay in bed
wanting
He lay in bed
beginning
He lay in bed
starting
He lay in bed
to die

THE RAPE OF LEDA
Joan Crate

Leda never knew time could bend
and languish like a swan's serpentine neck,
no crooks or breaks, only coils of wind-ruffled light,
and so she paused between wings and webs, girl
and womanhood, adrift
                        in a pool of dreaming.
A river of a bird pours promises in her ears.
Whirrs from the slender throat loop around her—
like the homilies of doves she thinks, tickled
by almost-sensations—water, clouds,
and love sonnets.
                    Feathers lap against her.
A quill scratches the high-water mark along one thigh.
She stiffens but doesn't want to misinterpret
or over-react, to pull from the premonition
of Eden blooming through her mind, its water lilies,
birdbaths, and feral teeth
                        used only for smiling.

She smiles and da Vinci paints her.

The swan's beak pushes between her legs.
She had thought it made of 24-karat gold,
the swan's feet of spider-silk and oranges.
Instead she feels a raptor's crude horn
and the scrape of barnacles across her belly.

Her gaze widens—a canvas stretched in all directions.

The afternoon tears open a typhoon—
bruised fists and webbed feet pummelling.
Gurgles of blood rise to the surface.
Leda's lungs fill. Frantic, fighting
she sinks beneath her story.

In the Uffizi Gallery, thick limbs of shadow
wrestle the artificial lighting.
Stroked in oil, Leda's rape has slipped away.

Gilt-framed, holding her swan, she lies,
across the canvas, the paint
on her silence cracking.

NORMALIZED
Jesse Holth

What are you doing?

My brain is foggy
I think my eyes are
closed

yes, they're closed
he thinks I'm
asleep

* * *

It comes to me every so often
I've had the realization before

I try not to think about it

too much

but I wonder

is it the same
for every

woman?

I have never told anyone

* * *

most of my friends
at university were
guys

in our group
I was often the only
woman

I never felt
unsafe
in any way
we were close
we cared
about each other
they were **good** people

* * *

it's late
we've all been
drinking

we are at someone's house
and we're tired
from the party

I'm lying down
on the couch
with two of my
friends

everyone is passing out
I'm mostly asleep

no one else is awake

we are all scattered
sleeping

I know **he thinks**
I'm sleeping

he slides his hand
down my shirt
under my bra

and **gropes** me

I don't move
I pretend
to be asleep

I don't know what to do
and I'm
confused

. . .

it's almost morning
when everyone leaves
we all say goodbye and
he hugs me

* * *

there are three
of us
watching a movie

when it's over
one friend leaves

he has to go
I can't remember why

I'm either
too broke
or too drunk
to make it home

I decide
to sleep there
no big deal

I didn't think
twice
about it

except now we're
alone

. . .

it's a large bed
should be
plenty
of room

we've all slept
in the same bed
many times

nothing weird about it

I'm trying to sleep
but he keeps
inching
closer to me

I'm not sure why

I rearrange
and move away
closer to the edge
of the bed

I start to fall asleep
but he begins
moving
closer again

he doesn't leave
me alone

I move to the couch

In the morning
I leave

I don't say anything

...

looking back
I remember

this one
had also made jokes

"**you would like it**"

* * *

we are celebrating
a friend's birthday

he has a cabin
where we've all been
many times

we go for the weekend
it's a beautiful
getaway
from the city

INNOCENCE / EXPOSURE — 35

. . .

we are drinking
playing games

I need some air
so
I decide
to go for a walk

my friend
joins me

it's dark outside
but he knows
the path
like the back of his hand

he helps me
down a steep
embankment

we are laughing

he gives me
a piggyback ride
down
the rest of the hill

I yell at him
not to drop me!
he's going too fast!

but
I trust him
and he doesn't
let me down

we make it
to the bottom
and walk along the road

side by side

we lie down
on the ground

to look at the stars
like we always do

they're so bright
there
we are talking
then he kisses me

he knows I have a
boyfriend
I remind him

we talk some more

he kisses me again
I tell him I can't

I end up
apologizing
to him

It's his birthday
and I feel bad

* * *

I don't know
why
they felt

entitled to my body
my body

why
no means yes

why
this is normal

why
I thought

"this is normal"

for so long
I don't think
I'll ever know
why

and
I have no
doubt

every woman has these
stories

or worse

even if they don't
realize
it yet

even if it's still
"normal"

even if their
friends
are good people.

TRY ME
Jo Jefferson

Dance floor knocked sideways by the seventh glass of draft
heat rising to knees, pelvis. Some yuppie bar hitching my
skirt a little higher with each round surprised by boldness a
lemony salty summery thing. It's June. Everyone's hot.

He's close enough for me to lean against then outside
shadows blurring all down Duke Street or Prince pressed against me the
edge of something digging in my back, legs jelly not desire anymore only
drinking and dancing too long and the smell of fish overwhelms me
still sloppy-kissing me, pantyhose full of holes now anyway.

Hearing my friend and her catch of the night moaning her
yellow hair lovely laughing face. This guy figures he got the ugly one
just another hard zipper against my leg no talk of protection from
boredom or neglect or hating myself. Nothing to offer except

the easiest sacrifice, this body strong enough to hoist a canoe
through a spruce bog tonight its only power to make some boy
change his mind about what his mother told him change his mind
about his taste in girls make him want to try me at all costs.

SIX MINUTES OF SPRING
Shannon Kernaghan

You, middle-aged and married, wormhole eyes, oozing syrup smiles that make my stomach clench. Me, twenty and eager, fertile bud of spring creating a grown-up name for myself, my career. You say, wanna feel like a million bucks? I say, no, but I wanna make a million bucks. My false laughter fast-walks me to your closed office door. I gasp for cool breezes of April to stroke my cheek, instead hard fingers clamp my shoulder, determined. You block my exit with your thigh and briefcase, push me down, and ignore my squeal—foreign noise—time now measured by the metronome hammer of my heart, maybe yours, hostile struggle on this rough-napped field of battle. How wrong you are, your million-dollar offer, with six minutes of defeat that steals my eager, ruins my spring, leaves me feeling like loose change dropped against a curb.

THE ELEPHANT
Marion Mutala

"It changes who you are." That is what Oprah says
It changes who you become
Evidence noted in a close relative
Perpetrator... another relative
The facts are true
Relatives assaulting relatives

It happened, so long ago
A mere child
Yet it eternally becomes "the elephant in the room"
Stomping, breaking souls, hurting, an inconsolable anger
"Confront the perp" counsellors say
Expose them

Sure, sure, sure
I have witnessed *those* results
The elephant always hungry, roaming
Grows and grows and grows

ENDURANCE / PERSISTENCE

Me, even in the dark, saying no.
—ELIZABETH JOHNSTON

NIGHT CLASS
Taryn Hubbard

Drudge street
dry wring
loose skirt
hem to finger
tips affix fists, ready.

Flatten tatter
city fragments
turn off ear
buds, listen soft
hey-you.

Zip up, step up
shoulders back towards
beautiful enough
side swipe
shadow creep.

Call your friend
call your mom
call your wonder
listen to the tone,
ask gently, *how are you tonight?*

Jaywalk sprint, cross
empty lot look
then eyes
forward. When the Buick
slows, run.

In tonight's class you read
of women in distress—
loves, flames. On
the radio you learn anything
can be a weapon,
even your house key.

A DEATH SO CLOSE
Rosemary Anderson

I wish I could have told you
Mum
while you were still alive

what happened
when I left for that new job
right after Daddy died

so full of empty.

How can it take so long
I asked the priest
for grief to fade?

I'd never known
a death so close
before
I told the priest

Is it okay he said
to hold your hand?

Of course I said
naïve
unschooled
unbelieving priests
could do such things.

How could I not
have known
how not
have just said *No* and fled far fast?

Terror frozen
in his murderous advance

no place to hide or run
no one to tell

no one to say who
was wrong
who
the victim wronged

no one to know

till one day
breaking
briefly free
I broke my secret
to the church High Priest

who told me
if I stayed
they'd crucify me
crucify me
crucify!
till I became
insane.

Forty years condemned
to my Hell
fraught with fear

I went
disgraced.

The priest they sent
to just another place.

I wish I could've told you
Mum
before you passed away.

THE NEXT DAY
Suzanne Wood

the next day you wake up before dawn
the top of your skull sore, tender to touch
after being thrust into the door handle
of the interior of the Pontiac Grand Am

the next day you slide out of bed
tiptoe to the bathroom in crunchy stained lace panties
molten branding-iron seared genitals
inner thighs show thumb prints magenta and blue

the next day you walk down the hall
your neighbour winks, says what he saw
steamy glass windows in the parking lot at midnight
you wish he might have stopped, knocked, rattled the door

the next day you try to count, possibly forty-eight
the number of times you said no
at first out loud, then silently as your ribs crushed
into the seatbelt buckle lying on the upholstery beneath you

the next day you remember being twelve years old
your aunt cooking nearby, on the other side of the wall
your uncle tickling you, touching your miniscule breasts '"accidently"
your reflex giggles, your shrieks of no— stop—help—please no

the next day you remind yourself
it was not until you kicked over your auntie's coffee table
three pinwheel crystal candy dishes, sliding, smashing, shattering
that she appeared, spitting out at you: "look what you have done"

A VICTIM
Carol Alexander

Having once chosen the convent, her flesh isn't spared.
Only a red shoe, its courtly heel trapped, lies awry in the evidence bag.

He was a teenage boy, she a woman edging into grey,
entangled in an alleyway at dusk that falls so early on a winter afternoon.

What does she remember of the incident?

The rumble of a subway train, quivering fog. The odd warmth of December,
my coat worn open, the almost musical cries of children in a tree-ringed mall.
Why I'd left as a novice, my sorrow not for heaven, but for my sake.
The martyrdom of St. Lucia and the gentle ox; his sword in me.

How for a year, avoiding mirrors, she'd learned to comb her hair,
but not to smile except in private at a bird or flowering tree.
Brilliant in the sacraments among pews of yellowed wood,
she stayed invisible to boys congealing into men.

What words did he offer in that sunless row of brick?

That he'd kill me if I struggled, and I believed.
Though I think now that even he was scared.
Then the speech was all our bodies, their mute apologies:
a little wider, I can't, just a little more. An initiation rite.
And the crimson heel, what she'd never before dared, buckled
under their double weight, and she was torn and lame.

In the clinic, wrist broken, she fumbles for her insurance card.
When asked, there is no one anywhere that she would wish to call.

BRAIN WASHING
Ronnie R. Brown

Today, women know
they shouldn't wash their body,
their clothes; are assured they *will*
be believed, but, back then,
she did what felt right: bathed, then
showered, then bathed again (while
her clothes soaked in the sink), sure
that getting rid of every trace—washing
it all away—would help her forget.

What use alerting the campus cops
her roommates argued. She'd been
where she shouldn't have been; was
drinking (under age); was (oh-
so-willingly) making out with him.
So what if he shoved her down
onto a mattress, parted
her thighs by pounding them
with his fists (whispering, as he did,
that he had military training, could—
would—kill her if she screamed.)

Later, bruised, but squeaky clean,
she sat on her bed, mug of tea
in hand, hair still dripping, hearing
his voice in her mind saying
what he'd said when he finished.
Hissing, "You weren't worth
the trouble, bitch—doing it alone
would have been more fun!"
His words repeating again and
again as she wondered what
she could do to wash him
out of her head.

I DON'T LIKE TO TELL PEOPLE I WAS RAPED
Elizabeth Johnston

It embarrasses. How could someone like *me*
get raped? It better be a good story. The kind

that makes you shiver. Like a stranger in a dark alley holding
a knife. Or an uncle when I was five. That's
something. That's really something

to feel bad about. Not how it actually went down.
How I partied all night with friends, kept drinking and they left
but I kept throwing back shots, my mini-skirt and me

doing handstands in the living room and all those guys, all
those guys waiting, counting. One more shot. Take
one more shot. Just one more. That's it, honey. That's a good

girl. Until I couldn't stand. Until it all went black. Just
faces haloed in fog. Me, sure, even in the dark, it wasn't what I wanted.
Me, even in the dark, saying no.

THE MORNING AFTER
Samantha Fitzpatrick

My eyes fight to open onto
the pale gloom of an unfamiliar room.
Daylight crawls through cracks in vinyl blinds.
My stomach quakes under the sudden weight
of nighttime Liquid Cocaine decisions.

I stumble down an endless hallway
into the arms of the bathroom sink.
I shrink at the sight of the mirror.
It glows beneath the vanity's uneven light,
illuminates only half of my face.

The faucet's cool touch is enough
to steady my nauseous shake.
Still, I press its handle back.
It runs blue and my knuckles ache
in their frigid baptismal state.

I sprinkle the imagined holy-water cure
over my smeared-makeup face.
I rub my cheeks with my wet palms,
dig my fingers into my cheekbones.
I wait for grace, but nothing comes.

The bar soap sits in an oily dish
thick with another's mistakes.
I circle it over my skin, as if its
milk-white lather could erase
another stranger's acid touch.

And what about the taste?
I jam the bar into my mouth.
It scrapes against my teeth.
I fight off the urge to retch,
commit myself to cleanliness.

But still I taste the alcohol, his tongue,
his sweat. Still I feel his body pressed
against my dead weight.
I spit the soap into the basin below. I heave,
but nothing else comes out.

BIRDMAN
Byrna Barclay

The man arrives dressed all in black,
the name of the company over his breast
pocket stitched in red: **ABLE.**

He totes a bucket and bags and bottles,
beneath his black cap and feathery hair,
hooded lids, the sharpest of hooked nose.

The mouth gives him away,
a wide slash, set hard.
His oval eyes dart and take in all

the pigeon droppings on the balcony floor,
the streaked glass, the smeared barbeque,
the bright-eyed male and three others

on the railing, like henchmen,
and the sight of him diving through the double doors
sends them into lift-off. He swoops into the corner

and reaching with one gloved hand
seizes the nesting female by the neck,
choking off a single breath,

his back to me now, a flutter of feathers,
his free hand holds the black garbage bag
the bird inside, silenced.

He tells me the male will return,
searching for his mate. I watch the birds
wing from the SaskPower building

to eaves under the hotel roof.
The birdman tells me they are just like us,
the best part of a man is a woman,
her softness.

CHANCE ENCOUNTER IN THE URANIUM CITY HOTEL
Marion Beck

Do you remember
that solicitous and charming man
chatting me up
as though I were a queen
to whom he should pay homage
till you came in
when he changed personality
became edgy
rather blustering
slightly protective
as though he thought
you might contaminate me?

It seemed unimportant at the time
a small incident to be brushed off
like a white hair on a black sweater
yet I suppose it was the first crack
in the rose-coloured glasses
placed so firmly on my nose
in school in the old country
where I'd been fed stories
of noble savages in a pristine wilderness
stories sprinkled as liberally as salt
on an under-seasoned stew.

But the stew proved tainted after all
and salt could not hide the flavour
anymore than it can truths
still surfacing today
like the bloated corpses of caribou
emerging through sick ice
at breakup.

I ACHE
Maroula Blades

I've been aching since the day I was born,
Dropped bloody by a nurse in the hospital
Ma spine's crooked; I just missed being dense.
Ma brother's good to me, talks to me he does.

I've been aching since the day I was born,
I asked ma uncle if I was pretty,
He said, "Let me feel you where you grow,
Lawd, you're pretty all right like a plump peach."

I've been aching since the day I was born,
Mama shoved me in the attic, visitors came,
I was scared. I was cold. I hate ebony spiders.
I waved coldly to people's backs through cracks.

I've been aching since the day I was born.
I asked a well-dressed priest, "Why is it so?"
He said, "God works in mysterious ways,
His ways are not our ways."

I've been aching since the day I was born,
Aches as I scrub Mr. Dixon's floor for coins,
Aches as I wring Mrs. Bell's sheets for nothing,
Battle aches as Joe touches me, his "beast gal."

Aches, one dull, heavy ache after another,
Scaly hands, bent bones, nothing but gruel.
I'm gonna hang this ill-fitting skin out to dry,
Go around bloody doing Carrie take-offs.

I'm gonna jump into the skin of a zebra,
Lovely like a Zulu shield, spear red soil with ma breath,
Back strong against the brawny wind,
Eat plenty; stamp mangrove with ma hooves, free.

A METAPHOR
Jill M. Talbot

I cannot tell you what happened because
I was not really there and he was wearing
a mask, he was someone else so really I knew we were
just dreaming, and when the wine spilt, red soaking
into the new carpet it was just
a metaphor on top of a metaphor, and the bruises
would surely go away since it was all, we know,
pretend. I played dead because no one really dies
in a dream, and he nodded that he'd play the boogeyman because
horror movies only live on the screen,
and we'd forget until one day I was writing a letter
and the ink spilt out like blood and his mask dissolved
and I was naked again.

SOLITARY
Marina Nemat

In my solitary confinement cell
A box of darkness
Or maybe a spinning sphere
My grave
Minutes are eternal
A breath lasts until the end of time
Further
Further
Further
Expanding
Knowing that I've been forgotten
I can't remember the butterflies and seasons
My heartbeat gnaws at my veins
Bleeding
Bleeding
Bleeding
But death has left this prison
I abandon my body
I have to
Its memory of itself fades
I float beyond pain and agony and their measures
Buoyant
This is a black Dead Sea
That is neither dead nor alive
No emotion escapes this realm
Heavier than time and gravity
Than all energy and soul and thought
When my interrogator lies on top of me
I feel the burning between my legs
But it somehow doesn't matter
Distant
He has spelled out my nothingness
And it transforms me bit by bit
Into cold drifting dust.

PULP NON-FICTION
Janis Butler Holm

He has stepped from a dark waiting place. He has moved toward her body with the crude insistence of a bad plot.

Her mind is stopped. She is fixed in the wisdom of stories learned too well: Be calm. It is inevitable. Do not struggle. He will only hurt you more.

For one long moment she stands mute, without motion. She could die of suspense. Then (here's the reversal) her pen is in her hand and stabbing through his flesh.

Unhappy ever after, she will live to confess how the fury in her throat exploded red and harsh and howling.

This story, like the others, is ugly and raw. It speaks a kind of wisdom. If I ask why we have such stories, such wisdoms, will I breach some artful code? Will I violate some expectation?

WOODS WOLF GIRL
Cornelia Hoogland

That girl in her story tight

as bark to a tree. A fucked girl, a violated girl, a girl red
with sex, a girl who asked for it, who suffered,
who liked the way he looked. A hyphenated girl,
a co-conspirator, a victim.
A used girl, a useful girl, a commodity

that sells. A wolf-girl,
a soul-bird, a lamb—

always more

than these glimpses, she is
a plot as
liquid as mercury she pours
from the broken thermometer and rolls in her palm.

If there is to be a rescue
let her, in this dark moment,

                    be it.

Let her enter the forest
                 the better to see

                 the depth
                 she's being offered.

P.O.ED
Halli Lilburn

I hang my head down. Hair, curled to impress, dropping over my face. Sucking in air like cheap drugs. Laughing adolescent Christians look on. Now they hold my neck against a wall and plug my nose, waiting for the oxygen to leave my brain. There are hundreds of faces with eyes swimming black. Two seconds and I am crouching in an alley hiding from a shadowy figure. Sweeney Todd is chasing me in Sherlock Holmes's London. Grey fog and shivering cold fingers. I scream through closed lips. There is that sucking sound again, and laughter under water. "Wake up!" My frozen body suddenly resurrected and I swing widely at my attacker. "What was that?" I'm back at the party and nobody knows what I saw but me. Still, they wonder at the weird noises I made. Is that what my unconscious mind is doing to me? Filling me with terrifying men?

A GOOD THING TO KNOW
Myrna Garanis

how many days it takes a bruise
to heal. Six for a thumb, for example.
The first day, nothing. Purple
swells into bloom around day two.

Say you're testifying, an insurance expert
or some such thing, you conclude
with certainty that five days have passed
since the thumb incident.

Bumps on the head take longer,
depending on velocity or force.
A yellow period lasts past a week,
as does the black-eye stage,
along the upper lids.

I'm not saying you have reason
to use this information. A bruise
is a fact like any other. How it happened
enters into the realm of fiction.

"WHAT WE DID NOT KNOW IN 1972. WHAT HAS CHANGED."
Penn Kemp

It's too late. He has jumped me, fallen on me, almost as
in love, catching his weight in his hands as they smack
against the grungy linoleum tiles I've wanted to replace.

The kitchen wall is rippling. The chalky ceiling bulges
as if it needs new plastering; as if something is trying
to pound through, something that can't be contained.

A flash flood, a fire? My spine slams against the door.
My skull is permeable. I know what's going to happen.

I don't know what's going to happen. Time expands to
include all the random possibilities of thought, of world.

Tectonic plates collide. I know that he erupts explosively,
a system under great pressure from without, from below.

His face balloons massively through the mist. I know him.
I know that drawn-down mouth, mask of Greek tragedy.

How often I have traced the dimple in his chin, a line from
nose to mouth where God pressed His finger: *the philtrum.*

His fingers close, blunt tips touching, the heels of palms
meeting as if in prayer. Relentless hands ring my throat.

Gold wedding ring presses deep into my gullet. Even in
absolute panic, my body responds to his closeness, dearly

familiar and almost kind. My breath stops, is stopped. My
breath holds itself, forgets itself under his thumbs, then

gasps. And is forced quiescent.

I have already disappeared up the smoky trail, out the top
of head into wide blue sky. A buzz as of bees in the cool

expanse of air. Strange croaks seem to start in my gullet
and travel up with me into the vast and empty. I am flying.

Mewling, I hover, open my new eyes to glimpse our roof, so
puny from this height. Beyond him, beyond myself, above.

*

Violent shaking startles me out of freedom: a sudden updraft.
I'm being pulled down the vortex of consciousness back into

a body I thought I'd surrendered. The sound in my ear, carol,
carol, and no song but choking, roaring. Nothing but his voice,
loud as Poseidon in a seashell in my ear. He's really done it now.

I swim in an ocean of blood. Swirling red currents fill each cranny
of consciousness and this time I go under, diving, divining down.

When I emerge, he is gone but the room is swirling around me
in colours of other travels. Turkish scarlet cushions. Moroccan

striped curtains dance a jig of molecules that confuse my senses.
I am lying on the couch. I shut my eyes again, not to see. Not

to hear. His footsteps, running closer. Water, soaking my head.
I look at him. A yellow cast of fear lies over last red flares of rage

on his face. But the hands that hold the basin barely tremble. "If
you've quite recovered," he announces, his voice oddly strangled.

"I'm off to town. Just take it easy. You'll be all right!" He commands. Irony of statement, concern of question or relief: it doesn't matter.

Pain neatly divides head from shoulders. Voice creaks like something inanimate outside its box. Words, the ability to make words—gone.

Phrases flutter and dissolve. "I'll be all right." Something automatic, something ancient in me, is attempting re-entry. "All right. Just go."

He is already gone, a flash of yellow bike. Silence except for that buzz of wasps in my head. Wasp-words ring in my ears.

*

Can either of us remember what it had been about this time? His jealousy of my phantom lover, the one that got away . . .

Who knew for sure what happened. What is this complicity between us? Already it's as if nothing at all had happened.

We can talk to no one, certainly not each other, about the sudden black holes, the mind-fields in ordinary conversation that suddenly erupt. Because most often,

they are not there. The house is simply a house, the scene domestic with cat and kids, and cauliflower on the stove.

I can talk to no one. I cannot talk. When I tried—family or friends—all told me that it was none of their business. Not to interfere. Not to know. I made my bed. Now lie in it. Lie.

When I did call the police, they listened intently to my story. "Is the perpetrator your husband, ma'am?" "Yes." "I'm sorry.

We do not interfere in cases of domestic assault. Thank you
for calling the Precinct." The dial tone still rings in my ears.

And where could I go anyway, on my own with two kids
and no money and a body that will not move. Shame—I

wrap it around me to keep warm as if it were my own,
protecting me from the eyes of neighbours, hiding black

and yellowing bruises under sleeves and stockings. What
have I done? Dishes, drying in the sink. What has he done?

The fingers I've studied so closely, bald sentinels drumming
action. Beating to their own rhythm, the jazz that syncopates

sudden movement. My glasses hang by a wire arm, frame twisted.
Retribution, then contrition. Pain is finite after all. He comes back

begging. I pride myself on the ability to forgive that's been bred
into me. A flip of power and I get whatever I want; he does whatever I want. Until resentment steams over again. Next time. No.

There will be no next time. There's never going to be a next time.
This I believe on faith. This he believes on faith. When he returns

after the kids are asleep, he knows he has changed, knows his ire
has disappeared forever, as if it never was. I know there is no more

fear. I pray there is no more fear. We hold onto each other all night.
without a word. Stealthily, while his breathing deepens, I practise

opening and closing my throat for when the words come. If I could
speak. For when I will speak. My jaw creaks on its wrenched hinge.

ENDURANCE / PERSISTENCE—67

*

His thumbs are imprinted on either side of my windpipe like black sentinels. For days, I wear a long turquoise scarf and go around

pretending I am Isadora Duncan. Pretending I could fly. Secretly, unwinding my scarf, I inspect the delicate progression of bruises.

A circle of yellow surrounds the thumbprint. I think I can make out the actual whorls that are the perimeter. Black fades to purple, then

softens to a yellowish centre. In the mirror, that face that is not mine looks out at me from the telescoped distance of time, wrinkled thin

with the patience of years. Her eyes clear and almost wise, assuring— she is somebody I will become, the face I will grow into someday.

HONOUR KILLING: A GLOSA
Troni Y. Grande

Oh, I wish I'd come over here once in a while!
That was a crime! That was a crime!
Who's going to punish that?

—Susan Glaspell, *Trifles*

Just before Canada Day
Honour drove Mohammad, the Crown alleges,
Father, son, wife number two
To overkill—daughters, sisters, "auntie" (wife number one)—
Bruise the voluptuous skulls, screw drugs between scarlet lips,
    drown and drown again
Four freedom-loving women ("treacherous whores," his words
    echo at the trial).
Canada's citizens line up to have a view. Beautifully *Maclean's*
    frames them,
Pierced and painted bodies stuffed in the black Nissan,
    bloated with family shame.
Did any Montreal neighbour watching on TV the monstrous
    mother in denial
Whisper up at the torture house, *I wish I'd come over here once in a while?*

Moist air hangs heavy, shimmers on Kingston waters.
The body remembers. I am the age of Sahar, floating free.
Once more I pull before dawn short shorts and pop-top over
Uncharted curves, discipline the body I am barely learning to love,
Head down past Frontenac County Court House,
Feet drumming cobblestones on Princess Street,
    thighs proud with blood, in time
To watch the sun light on lapping rocks, hear the birds begin their warm-
    breasted catechism.
One morning a woman materialized
    under a waterside oak, poised on a flat-topped rock,
Blue hijab billowing. I snapped her photo, arrested the sublime,

ENDURANCE / PERSISTENCE—69

Not knowing the power of the gaze. *That was a crime.*

By a human hand the upper and lower locks, Kingston Mills
Gush open. A world away, we chat about an other body.
I plant elbows on the seminar table, worn and decent,
    congratulate my self.
My students warm to Shakespeare's dying heroine,
The woman stained, dishonoured, drained,
Catalyst for the hero's journey. Does *Titus* stand the test of time?
Did rash Andronicus do well to slay his only daughter?
    Yes, they argue, Lavinia had no use,
Lopped and alien, speechless, what life was hers?
They make a sacrifice what I thought to call a murder,
    cut down the daughter in her prime,
Stop their ears against my protest—but *that was a crime!*

July again. The ferry ride is over.
We've seen the sights, a family on vacation,
Cooled by the breeze off the water,
We step off the ramp onto the stifling pavement
A stone's throw from Kingston market, grey courthouse in the distance.
A cattle truck waits by an eatery. I turn my head to look at
The unearthly sound. A cry to sting our nostrils,
The smell of penned creatures knowing their brutal end.
As we pass by, one fringed brown eye through the metal slat
Catches me in its circle, sears my memory, this infant moan:
    Who's going to punish that?

Words for "no" in over one hundred languages.
—KATHERINE LAWRENCE

RAGE / RESISTANCE

AN ARMY OF STARING WOMEN
Susie Berg

—*compiled in part with words from Sue Goyette and friends*

My heart is sore, the way the women's testimonies have been left to stew; the private way they coped made public. There is a great dishonouring, me wrapped in a skin stitched of pins, pricking like the first sweater I knit and insisted on donning even though truth be told it was nearly painful to wear. I want to try something different like banging out "R.E.S.P.E.C.T." on pots and pans on the stoop in front of my house as though all the noise I will ever make could be gathered and roared out just this once. I am saying, and not only in the unarmoured rooms of my mind: "angry," and "frustrated," and demanding to know why this judicial system thinks only virgins are incapable of lying. I am repeating "angry," and "sad," and then pressing my fingers against a small, new shoot of hope that we are edging that day when voices echo. We are wounded, but we feel hope. We toggle between optimism and deep sorrow, return to the same old same old, back to words never spoken so publicly, back again to how much work there is. When will it end when will it end. And then I shake that off and put my shoulder to the boulder again because what the hell else? Back and forth, back and forth, I can't find words in the muck and the fog. The songs of late-March birds outside my window wake me early every morning. At bedtime I misdirect my anger at them, forgetting that the nighttime noises are crickets and the birds are long quiet. My shoulders are too burdened, so I've walked, wept, listened to frogs in the spring mud. We are all in the same room together, yes, and all the women's voices are announcing: This is what sexual assault looks like. This is how women respond. This, and also this, and this, too. There are more unmistaken reverberations than fallen leaves on the forest floor, than the tendrils of briar that reach out and choke my knees as I pick my way along the shale outcrops into the Boyds Mill creek, than there are fingerprints on permanent file, impressed in the hollow just above my collarbone or between my legs. Maybe one day a match will be declared. I am doing a kind of prayer, a ritual like nothing I ever saw my grandmother execute on Sunday mornings in church. Watch, compare, look away. Watch, compare, look away. Watch. There's nothing happening here that isn't happening somewhere else. The only difference is that now I'm watching.

FUCK GHOMESHI
Lori Hanson

A Tribute to Lucy's Courage

Lucy DeCoutere did not know what hit her when Marie Heinen called her to the stand three days early. The crown and her lawyer had ill-prepared her for the onslaught of questions. The Canadian public read about Lucy in a way that painted her as scattered, as a liar, as confused, and as vindictive. In an interview for *Chatelaine* magazine after she had testified, her own words revealed more of the person. In that interview, Lucy says:

> I can't live with this the way it is right now. There has to be something positive which comes from this. When I first went into this experience, it was like "Get Jian to stop hurting people." Then my focus changed. Instead of dwelling—as I will do, on what happened personally—**there's got to be a better way to fix the system. Maybe we can use this awful opportunity to make a bit more of an even playing field.** [my emphasis added]

Personally I feel Ghomeshi deserves no more attention, fame, pity or glory. Lucy, though, deserves to be really heard—if not in court, then by us, the Canadian public. So Lucy, this is dedicated to you, and to all the women with the courage to try to speak out about sexual assault.

A Rise-up Chant

The post-traumatic haze
from memory's mislaid years
True story not well told
Court vultures rapt—all ears.

Ghomeshi's got the class
to punch and fuck and choke
No fear of repercussion
the legal show's a joke.

We're told the scam is just
the system's working right
Just turn your heads away
no point in seeking fight.

The jails are full and mean
creating more of them:
The hateful breed of man
that dreams of power again.

We do what we must do
Our legal route is warped
The streets are out there waiting
Chants—our last resort.

To be shouted, preferably on the street, by a large group of women-supportive non-violent people.

FIVE PARTS RAPE POEM ONE PART SELF-CARE
Kyla Jamieson

know better
than to go out
if you do
go to a friend's
don't wait
for your boots
to dry
they won't
& you can't
lift the chill
if you try
or wish or ask
or insist
rain will fall
the mechanism
is ambiguous
no one
has studied it
with research
council dollars
the way they have
the pay gap
or performance
of gender
even when
the invisible
becomes visible
the rain
will still call
you insane
numbers
are one thing
optics another

there are
so few planes
where they meet
in the aisles
& drink tiny
bottles of booze
the flight attendant
says aloha
the pilot
rapes her later
what comes after
a line
with rape
in it?
I guess
what comes after
is what comes after
I've heard
gossip saves
& want to name
all the sleazebags
probable rapists
the kind
you might date
you accidentally
say OK
after they rape
you but also
might not
it takes all kinds
long list short list
crown the rapist
but I'm scared

plus I've been
such a bad
bad girl
like already
I've used the words
rape & rapist
too many times
in this poem
it's 2016
& jian's not guilty
but my
credibility's shot
hey
let's take a break
how are you
feeling?
lately I can't sleep
I put stones
on my chest
& try to remember
oregon coast
pacific surf
sand-flecked wind
salting my body
spinning wildly
no one calling me
crazy so subtly
that even I
& even you
wonder
is she?

THE POWER IN A NAME
Heather Read

You did
You did you did
You did that to me
There was no name for it then that didn't conjure blame
of me when

You did you did you did that to me

A girl of thirteen who befriended you
attention-seeking, sweetly lost at sea
green
her tiny power wielded with eyeliner
But you took that away, when you did

you did you did you did that to me

Like plucking a flower who begins to wilt
upon the plucking
And you oblivious in all your fucking

you did you did you did that to me

And to all the girls of thirteen who don't yet
own their sexuality
They believe it a pet they can use as they like
and leave behind when it doesn't serve them right
but more like a pet dragon whose will of its own burns the hand that feeds
And this is what you get when you mess with the big boys
This is what you said to me

The dialogues opened and never sated
The overturned beacons, storms in their wake
Don't deny don't be sly don't be nineteen

RAGE / RESISTANCE

I never came forward I couldn't be seen
If I had then I could expect that
The shame of all the others I'd done would be visible and used
To blame me for what you'd done.
What you'd done

You did you did you did that to me
A small moment of pleasure or power for you
A year's reckoning and shame for me

The awful belly-digging place that you laid bare
And I dug it worse than you ever could, after you'd been there
The landscape of my body used and disposed
like a clearcutting operation
Not a space spared
And your name rings and echoes endlessly
You deflated my fledgling dream and sucked my power out of me
Power wielded with black eyeliner and a trucker mouth
Or rather, you turned it inside out and it became a vacuum
    that depleted me

You did you did you did that to me
Like a visually stunted queen locked in a handmade tower
And never before have I said this aloud
That did you did you did that to me
But though I'm not alone I'm invisible in a crowd
The millions of women like me and the millions of men like you

Randy, now I own it and you do too
And this is what you get when you're thirteen and a slut and this
    is what you get when you're forty-four and stuck

Randy, I own it and now you do too
And this is what you get when I speak your name for the magic
    that speaking will do
Randy, you did
You did that to me
and to every other girl you did it to, you did to her and I stand and call it
Randy
Randyrandyrandyrandyrandy...

And after that now when I say your name
It rings mute and dead, heavy as lead
The echo chamber is lined with soft fleece
The echo is empty
And this is what you get.

A CONSIDERATION OF THE BUS DRIVER
dee Hobsbawn-Smith

She prefers to imagine him alone with his rearview mirror,
rows of empty benches and all-seeing windows
bearing witness, his seat a backless stool,
its spring uncoiling, corkscrewed metal
impaling him.

This is the only form of punishment
she has, all she can rely on to allay
the way his hands unsheathed themselves,
the coiling ligature of fingers, the lines they left
along her throat and thighs.

She sees the stool, a brushy spring
motionless, its penetrating
column emerging
from his mouth, as justice
she may never otherwise find.

THE MAID AND THE WOLF
Ashley-Elizabeth Best

I'll fight with all I have: time.

I'm always of two minds about everything.
Incubating the idea of life between my hips,
dividing cells satellite in unspilled blood,
the soaking burrow of his hidden hoard.

The truth is always terrible and boring.
My regard is equal to my fear.

When will someone notice my bravery
and call it terror?

Hair shackled to my throat, I am no longer
those who see my pain. I'm a fire consuming
all that came before me. In our lapsed understanding
the lines of his face read runic.

To go wrong in one's own body, cast the wishbone
of a bird, stencil your love's name on your breast,
swan your way through the lunar wet.

We are divided in this remembering.

I exile myself from the burning church of the body.
My bones fake the memory of flesh, offer their own
confused eulogy.

THE RAPE OF LUCIA
Keith Inman

Joseph bent to the fountain and let
the cool water wash over his face.
Behind him, the hard echoes of boys in a shower
fogged the change room, Jayse and Billie

turned rigidly
under the fury of cascading water, their voices
stifled in heat. Joseph
heard his sister's name.

He spat into the drain, beads dripping
from his forehead, and stood upright.
Jayse smiled at him, the horde churned
in red laughter. Joseph

strode across the wet floor to the toilets
and stabbed each silver handle
along the outside shower wall, each
porcelain lung choking with rushing water

from the main feed above. Steam billowed
into the tiled hall, "Fuck! Cock Sucker!"
screamed the boys as Joseph sat on the bench,
the towel twisting in his hand, and waited.

PINNED, MOUNTED
Amber Moore

It was too fucking cold to walk but I did it
anyway. I couldn't look at my hands without
thinking of his so I smashed them in my red pockets,
punching my sides as I stalked on. My elbows stuck out like wings.
Crimson felt beaded along my tank top, seeping out from thick seams.
His fingers were short
and meaty and always slightly shaking—so unlike
my own, which were still until I
pushed back.

He barely glanced up from *Halo* to
say hello. The moment I'd been sick over for
weeks seemed so anticlimactic that I forgot to be
relieved. He slumped and I stood, wishing I could reach into the
screen for that shotgun and push his heart back into
the couch that my hair was likely still threaded in. I
walk in submission to the back door. I notice my hands as I reach
    up for the knob;
They are red and swollen from the clenching.

CHRYSALIS
Lucie Kavanagh

When the social worker arrived,
I noticed a moth.
Lethargic heat flung by frantic wings.
Mirrors swam in the humidity
while she spoke and wings flailed.
Furious.
I watched my fingers tap a steady rhythm
on the windowsill, far away
from her words and the blankness
of their soft echo.
The whole world outside
was a rushing green silence.
You stood watching.
A stupidity in your stance made me shudder,
bent and blackened against the fierce red
of beaten-down rage.
There were no angry words, only drumbeats,
wings hesitant to return to the calmness,
aching for peace.
I stayed away.
Out of a dancing summer I made an island,
waves and boats and only in dreams
would they bring me under with them,
pulling breath, heart and soul.
I would press my hand to feel each bone,
to know sheer solidity.
Footfalls were only heartbeats.
No more games.
One day, reflected in raindrop fragments,
a dead moth,
life and breath pulled taut and dry.
You pulled a chrysalis tight around me,
closing in with warmth and darkness.
I disappeared.

Maybe you still see my footprints
in the sodden grass of early morning.
I still see yours
in my eyes.

CLAIMING MY BROTHER'S BODY
Keir

I should have come yesterday but I am here today instead while my children sleep in their shared bed, their door shut. I would have come two years ago, but our sister was visiting then and needed to settle things at last though some things can't be settled so you just let them go *but how can you tell, they could always come back* that's what she said.

A year ago Graham told me the way it was with him. I already knew, so what difference does it make? He buried a daughter the year we buried you. He never speaks of her—that was a long time ago, I was down east and couldn't come home so I walked the way you and I used to walk, for miles and miles, and when I found my way back it was as if I'd been gone for a long time with no forwarding address.

Where I am now, the blinds are made of paper. Rose-coloured. Here is the album with your obituary, the letter Bev wrote because you were still in hospital and weren't well enough to write. With my brand-new sense of responsibility and graduate degree, I said I'd come west in the summer, but too late. I had to borrow money to fly out to your funeral in February. Our family stayed in a hotel; no one came to see us. We went out for supper and Graham ordered cheap Portuguese wine, which was funny because the waiter brought a tasting glass.

The technician at the morgue said you were killed instantly and couldn't have suffered, but how can anyone know a thing like that. For ten years we hardly spoke, but your voice is with me—the doggerel you recited in the top bunk on 26th Street, the predictable meter honed with the vanity which helps me remember.

I am taller than you, I have a picture. No scar on your forehead yet. Only the blur of a gesture as you lean forward in the olive sweater you wore when you left, wore on the day you stepped onto the road in the rain. At last I have come. It is slow work, learning to see inside your body, the shattered spleen, the rib that caved in your lung. And our old friend, the wrong left between us.

LXVIII
Sonnet L'Abbé

Stupid truth. I must quit bullshitting myself. I cheat the workweek, fake the committed application of my days to productive work—I don't know why I circumvent beginning; almost automatically I balk; I have days and days until the deadline and suffer slowly—some errand, some random invitation always consuming me before the sober banalities of task—roundabouting, stressing, mentally scolding myself, suffering accusations from the better worker I mean to be—Procrastinating is an ordeal, an untrustworthiness of habit, groveling for a living—My brow begging, furrowed, I promise, this time, golden stretches of discipline, I will sow faithfully, blessed expanses of would-be—The spectre of foresight hovers, foreseeing applause, lynchings, boredom I caused, hollow praise, respect—How is respect even fathomable when I'm so nauseatingly beta? Even now my lines are avoidance, another second syllabified, another second phenomenalized in verse when syllabi remain unwritten—Everyone else does what needs flogging; while I sleep away decades, time advances another eager beaver, somebody else has it in him to choose methodical essay over le fantastique—the hours daydreamed at screens, twittering hours, I let them all go rotten, and mentally acquit myself, and spiritually perjure myself, making the obnoxious excuses all bums mutter, contemptuous of another's greed-driven mojo— I'm robbing someone, or something (a self I don't know, a lost address) and flushing the spoils before my inner authority can retrieve what's undone—Is this poem a justification, or a map, or do I pitch a new quality of manure? Let's just recognize that rapey buddy got close by showering you with false admiration. You wanted, sweetheart, to believe he saw authority in the small works you asked of yourself.

WHEN YOU LOOKED AT ME DID YOU SEE ME?
Ellie Rose Langston

Did you see my arms and think of how wildly they gesticulate
    when I'm telling a story?
Or did you see my arms and picture how you would use them
    to pin me down?
Did you see my lips and visualize how they must look when
    they're spread apart, smiling?
Or did you fantasize about your mouth pressed against them
    so hard as to muffle my scream?
Did you look into my brown eyes and ponder how they might light up
    as I watch the sun rise?
Or did thinking about how the tears would cascade down my cheek
    send a shiver up your spine?
Did you watch me tuck my hair behind my ear and remember
    how my mum would spend hours trying to tame it?
Or did you anticipate the power that you would hold over me
    as you used it to drag me towards you?
Did you look at my hands and see how I used them to guide
    my little sister across the street?
Or did you imagine how they would feel as you held them
    pressed against you?
Did you see my legs and picture how powerfully they carried me
    when I ran?
Or did you try to fathom how far apart they could be spread
    to accommodate you?
Did you look at my neck and see the small freckle, identical to the one
    worn by my best friend?
Or did you delight at visualizing your hands wrapped around it
    so tightly that I had to fight for breath?
And did you see me as a daughter? A sister? A friend? A human being?
Or did you simply see me as a collection of body parts
    that were yours for the taking?

Because now when I take a step back to behold myself in the mirror
I don't see my arms and think of all the friends that I held close
I don't see my lips and fondly remember my first kiss
I don't see my eyes and notice their depth
I don't see my hair and picture it billowing out behind me as I run
I don't see my hands and recall all the blades of grass
    that I have ran them through
I don't see my legs and commemorate all the places that
    they've carried me
And when I look in the mirror I don't recognize myself
Because when I look in the mirror
All I see is You.

ABUSE VICTIM
Marianne Jones

my rage is an inward thing:
instead of screams, silence;
instead of violence, furious stillness;
instead of striking out, i curl in
as rigid as hardened clay
as brittle as the firing makes it.
only the eyes, spitting ice shards, speak;
the eyes of a caged cat

NOT EVEN TREES SHOULD GROW THERE
Emma Lee

How long do buildings retain the sounds they absorb?
No matter how well-bleached the floors are underneath
new carpets, how sugar-soaped the walls beneath
new wallpaper, even when former furniture and linen
were taken and burnt, do echoes linger under the plaster?

Tourists are tempted by a forest lodge, walks in the woods,
fresh on-site facilities, a break from the bustle of town.
Their government insists nothing happened here,
an empty building has been brought back to life
to bolster a burgeoning industry.

Neighbours over a new country border
argue the site should be razed, that not even trees
should grow there, their greenery a betrayal.
The moaning the guests hear is not due to the wind.
That sob is not a floorboard settling,
that scream is not air trapped in a water pipe.

THE NO VARIATIONS
Katherine Lawrence

naï jo lass votch xeyir ez he na aïlle né nann
        ma hoke phu hmar te no tla hla pù shi nò ne ne nej nee
no ne ei nei ei no nee no non nanni ara nein ohi nahániri

non 'aole lo nahin nem nei mba tidak no iié ala thay oya
        ahneo no nab bo minime non nē no ţe nee neen ne tsia tidak
le kaore ugui nennin nei non nei нӕй no kheyr nie não na

nu нет niet no ag ne aiwa na nae nie ne ne aï no siyo hapana nej
        hindi aita illaï yuk kadha maï (maï chaï) hayir oevoel ug
ні hahin neni nage awa déedéet nein rara cha no

no(te)
Words for "no" in over one hundred languages, sourced from
https://www.freelang.net/expressions/no.php.

NAME ME AFTER A FISH
Leah MacLean-Evans

Goldeye or Cichlid
silver and smooth and genderless, make me
as an alien, forget
the rules, name me
Corydoras of two halves, name me Coelacanth
for surviving
name me Plecostomus
name me Trout
name me Catfish
let them imagine my genitals as smooth
tough skin, not think to touch them.
Say, let me introduce Pickerel.
Say, have you met my friend Haddock.
Say, this is my daughter Herring.
And I will breathe water in and through me,
swim flicking in the slip.

THE WAY THE CROCODILE TAUGHT ME
Katrina Naomi

I swooned at the large god of him, sunning.
A tooth for every day of my life.
He performed his run along the bank,
as males do. I brought my boat closer.
He took to following, at a distance.

I wasn't taken in, knew his four-chambered heart
pumped love out and in, in and out,
knew his tongue had few good uses,
knew all about his grin. Yet whoever said he was cold-
blooded has never truly known this beast.

He brought out the prehistoric in me. I dived.
We swam, belly to belly, to where the Niles meet,
tussled as we thrashed among the weeds. After, I lay
the length of him, a limestone lilo, studs patterning
my skin. He smiled at me, often. Taught me all he knew.

Years later, when a man tried to drag me under,
I practised the force my lover had held back—
levered my small jaws open to their furthest extent,
splashed them down on the human's arm.
My attacker still carries the mark of my smile.

MOLLY
Polly Johnson

It is you who confess to me this thing
that had happened to you,
a long time ago while I was at home,
probably worrying about you
because you were so wild,
so vulnerable, so clearly alone,
but how could I not have known?

You tell me between our eating cake
and washing up, prepared to go back
and do battle with the mess that is your room.
"I want to tell you something," you say,
your face falling somewhere
between five years old and grey.

And then you tell me: words I
cannot even now write down—
that make me want to take a knife
and cut, upwards and down,
sideways, letting the guts spill out,
hoping that crows will pull them out—
so that they suffer, and suffer long.

My precious one, that I so singularly made,
who wandered away from me towards that place.
I wasn't there, because you all let go,
leaving us to stand here,
while the scrapings from someone else's shoe
tread across our dreams.

. . .

We eat cake and because you are mine
I remind you that it wasn't you,
that it isn't ok, and that I love you.
While inside my whole being shrivels.
It will go on shrivelling for the rest of time.
There is no justice, there is never just one victim.
But here is this cake, and we eat it.

NOT GUILTY
Donna J.A. Olson

All eyes were on me,
All of them judging and cruel.
They were all hoping that I would screw up and flee,
Just wanting it done and to hear the judge's rule.

They call my name,
And I start trembling in fear.
I feel like I am to blame,
Since I am the whole reason we are here.

I take the stand and swear in my oath,
In a trembling breath I tell them all that I know.
The hateful words and touching that I loathe,
The violation that my body still showed.

The whole time he sat with a smirk,
A knowing in his eyes of everything that I told.
The outside was just a facade of the monster that lurked,
But it was an act that he completely sold.

I could tell by the faces gathered,
That believed in him and not me.
My whole world seemed to completely shatter,
When the verdict came back "Not Guilty."

AUTUMN IN THE EAST, THE PILOT
Jami Macarty

Not sky, but blue as in bruise

Oak leaves, maple leaves bird groundward

Her face a future plum mulch, eyes swollen shut

The birds forage, the leaves moulder

Fields brittle, air hoarfrosts

Geese less than south

Bread toasts in the small oven with a family of ducks painted on it

After she asks a question

She sees his hands thrust

Throttle her throat

She pitches, drops altitude

His rudder input keeps her flying straight ahead

Forward force into the kitchen wall

His dream since a boy to be a pilot

He *was* for American

Her daughter makes the correction

She formalizes complaints with the airline, the pilots union

She causes him to lose his captain's stripes

Without concern for his future, without regret

THE MAN WHO STUDIED LOVE
Bruce Rice

I must have been born with this wound; it took a while
for the blood to catch up.

I don't think I was weak. I loved to teach, wrote
books. I tried to put some good into the world.

But you, my son, murderer at twenty, rapist, erasing
everything I am. And, then, of course, *her*.

It should have been me with the placards down at Court
of Queen's Bench. Instead, I was home, the curtains drawn.

What father does not pity another
what a child sometimes does.

Now I am ashes, the shame of us both still blows
above this scorched, this frozen ground.

This is about evidence and the washing of clothes,
homosocial space

and screamers' *The fucking judge went fucking easy*.
It's about race and a hooker who wasn't so lucky—thirty bucks

for a blow job so you said you would
kill her *So do it*. She must have believed you.

This is about something missing, the furnace
you shoved me into.

This is my obituary, the decimal that comes
when a life stops at fifty-three the way mine did—the pity in the room

in the tributes of the colleagues and your name missing
in the space where it says *Survived by*, the insufficiency

of words
and the echo of a tin can being kicked without so much as

sorry ... sorry ...

YES, THOSE WERE CRIMES OF VIOLENCE
Marshall L.

Part 1

Shame
Shame
Shame
I'm the one to blame

I could never trust a word she said
Or the way she put me to bed

Voices in my head growing louder
But for the next twenty years I'll know silence

Her face was devilish
But this was the only affection I ever got

Teenage years rally past
I knew my silence couldn't last

Alcoholism, drug addiction, promiscuity
Can you see it yet?

Shame
Shame
Shame
I'm the one to blame

Now the voices in my head grow louder
I need help

Four years of therapy
Three years of sobriety
Two years of changed identity
And in One year I'm ready

Part 2

Waiting for persecution
To be shamed by this institution... and this is what I hear:
"The judge and the courts bear witness to the case of a child that came
 into this
world sinless. Subject to violations and tribulations. Subject to the touch
 of another
in ways and places inappropriate for a mother. So let this case be laid
 to rest with
testament made and verdict known, for a child put to the severest test
 who suffered
those years alone.
'Yes, these were crimes of violence. Yes, you were the victim'
... No more years of holding silence
... No more dreams of violence
We see and hear and believe you. We know this is real and although
 we can't change
it, we recognize the pain you feel."

Part 3

And now I've been financially awarded
For twenty years of growth being thwarted

And I'm grateful. I'm not as crazy as I thought I was.
I don't feel like I'm making it up anymore

Yes, those were crimes of violence
And yes, I was the victim
Yes, those were crimes of violence
And yes, I was the victim

You don't need to be alone anymore
You don't need to be alone anymore
I'm not alone anymore

WREATHS
Amy Sonoun

—*after George Herbert*

1
Today my daughter testified *de raptu meo*,
"Concerning my rape," bore witness to the truth,
The truth of that to which she testified,

From Latin *testis*, root of "testicles"—
In the vernacular, "*cojones*," "nads,"
"Balls," "boys," and "stones"—and though she swore by none,

No man or boy has call to lend her one.
Her one great role—played by so many stars!
So many stars, most cast for just one night,

For one-night stands, no second or third trial,
Trying, under pressure, to say what's right.
The right to silence generally conferred on us

Conferred, on her, an onus to speak up,
Speak up and stanch those tears behind her words
Her words could stanch. It's all obscenely trite,

To write a scene—cribbed from a screen—that writes
Itself, itself repeats and magnifies the harm,
The harm, not hurt, it took some balls to do.

2
Cecilia Chaumpaigne played her role. No balls,
But balls enough to testify that Chaucer,
Chaucer the couplet man, did take by force,

Did take by force what she alone might give,
Might give and never have again. Released—
By her released—he sent Cecilia ten pounds.

Ten pounds Cecilia gained for having "stones."
Chaucer's stones lie now in Poets' Corner.
In Poets' Corner canons dust his stone,

His stone and those of lesser English poets,
Poets whose voices dropped a pitch at twelve,
And who, by twelve, knew honesty by tone,

By tone of voice—the men who hear it, know it.
I know what silence in a church won't say,
Won't say which of these poets, pens at rest,

Penises dust, rests easily in such a place,
Placed as they are so close to Geoffrey Chaucer,
Chaucer the couplet man, stone silent, now as then.

3
Athens cross-examined Maycomb's Ewells,
You'll recall, in *To Kill a Mockingbird*,
A mocking, superior Atticus Finch

Inched Mayella Ewell away from perjury,
The jury itching to deliberate,
Deliberately to affirm Mayella's lies,

Lies she learned at the left hand of her father,
Farther and farther, bent by blows, from truth.
One "truth" witnessed on screen by many boys—

Many too many boys?—Mayella lied,
Lied like a girl, lied *de raptu sua*,
Concerning a "rape" that wasn't one at all,

But a confederacy—Maycomb's fathers'
Fathers' fathers bringing rope for that "boy" Tom,
Tom "robin's son," no mockingbird safe from Finches.

From Finches too many boys learned girls lie,
Lie ballsy with their right hands on the Bible,
Biblically lie about boys they know they want,

Want to lie *with*, not *to:* lie is what girls do.
Girls do not have what it takes to testify—
From Latin *testis*—*de raptu sua.*

4
How many met like Cecilia and Chaucer?
Chaucer in arras, whispering "boo," pen stiff,
Stiffened most urgently, though he was married,

Married fourteen years, and not to Cecilia,
Not to Cecilia but to a well-born maid
Called Phillipa, like her queen, a lady's maid

Made in a bed—her father a courtier,
And a courtier's son—a vessel, a lady
Made—doubtless—in release, release most blessed,

Blessed by the church, and with his wife ordained,
Ordained the one vessel of his seed. How many?
How many met like Cecilia and Chaucer?

Met Chaucer, and made him ache—so he did find—
And finding make, make in his chamber, make
To understand him, at a feast, in half-light

Half-cast and half-withheld by torches,
Torches, sconces, tapestries, or in some crook,
Crooked while his one vessel Phillipa danced her part,

Her part in a new reel, and rushed to enter,
To enter as he entered, in a rush, to reel,
And reeled, too, in a bawdy house, as some say

Cecilia's stepmother did run, as her family name,
Chaumpaigne, French for "open country," or "field"—
That field, as it were—seems made for meaning.

5
Today my daughter took Cecilia's part,
Mayella's part. For Chaucer stood a boy,
A boy my daughter "knows," but barely—

He barely knows her, though they've met, this boy,
The boy who got her stoned, the boy whose stones
Ached—she passed out—ached until they didn't.

I haven't said yet how he met my daughter,
My daughter, whom he knows biblically: she drank
Three shots, pre-party, then he put a bong

Bang against her mouth. Maybe they kissed, lips
Bang against lips. Maybe he put his hands,
His hands, on her ass, in his room. Maybe,

Maybe his balls ached, like Chaucer's balls, until—
Until they didn't. She'd passed out. When she woke,
She woke in open country, no underwear,

Nowhere near his room. She didn't know until—
Until she did. She does not know him sober.
Sober is Athens, not Maycomb. Sober can

Consent. Sober knows "no" and "no" is no
Double negative. Soberly she testified,
From Latin *testis,* meaning "stones," and "boys."

6

My mother held her tongue and held a glass,
A glassy silence seventy years long,
So long that even I learned to see through it,

See through the nothing that her mother made,
Made and kept for her, until she'd make her own,
Her own to care for—silence, a man, and children.

(Six children, it turned out, four of whom had balls.)
The balls it took to break so long a silence!
The silence brokered, weekly, by her mother,

Her mother, weakly, strengthening in mine
What I reject in me. Of course her mother knew,
Knew for years her husband raped her daughter,

Her daughter tasting beer and anthracite,
Anthracite, tobacco, and acid reflux,
Acid reflux, like emotion mooted,

Muted, his slow bent motion muting her
Mute bedsprings, release coming to nothing,
Nothing for seventy years, nothing I saw through.

RAGE / RESISTANCE—109

7
When my older brother raped my older sister,
My older sister says, I had just come out,
Come out—peekaboo!—like the film based on

To Kill a Mockingbird, starring Gregory Peck,
Star of *Roman Holiday,* my mother's leading
Leading man, who would not touch a lady,

The lady she wanted to believe she was,
And *was,* unless she wanted him. O Attic shape!
O Atticus, O Tom, unable to keep silent,

Silent as glass, as vodka with rocks, not stones,
Not testifying, from Latin *testis.*
My sister did not not not want to say it,

To say it is not Boo—is never Boo,
(Whose name means "be afraid")—it is not Boo
We ought to fear, but fathers, brothers, mothers.

8
A wreathèd garland of deservèd praise,
Of praise deservèd, unto thee I'd give,
I'd give to thee, who knowest all men's ways,

Men's crooked, winding ways, wherein we live,
Wherein we die, not live: for life is straight,
Straight as a line, and ever tends to thee,

My daughter, who did testify today
De raptu meo, and who does not write lines,
Nor poems, which sound so round but wind,

110—RESISTANCE

Wind down the page, as Herbert's "Wreath" has done,
Must do, in black and white, for poems' resemblances
Dissemble. Life is not straight. It writes,

It writes us down, twists facts, makes images.
Imagines, for example, a girl waking,
Waking up sober in life's open country,

Glassy eyes open and no clear memory,
Memory cleared by alcohol and life.
Life left grass in her hair. Life's strong left hand

Bruises the page, as any poem must do,
Must do, to do a poem's work—hurt and not harm;
Hit hard and drive the reader to her corner.

To corner a mockingbird's no sin, you know.
You testified, my daughter, *de raptu meo*,
"Concerning my rape." I have bent these wreaths

For thee, who art more far above deceit,
Than deceit seems above simplicity.
Forgive not poetry, but poems' complicities,

So I may live, and like, and know thy ways.
Know them and practise them: then I might give
For these poor wreaths, give thee a crown of praise.

YEARS TOO LATE
Ed Woods

Life after abuse
is no picnic
No "Movie of the Week"
or documentary to share
Just the facts that the abuser
lives in comfortable gloat

Maybe thirty years from now
hell, maybe fifty years
just like the Nazi perpetrators
They finally become accountable
while on some government pension

Abusers have a support system
even from jail
But they have a greater reward
in the fact that accountability hides
Hidden deep until time no longer matters

Now found out in truth
old and broken
with sympathetic apologies
It is too late to look at survivors
directly in their eyes

Somewhere a court will end up
with a decision it is pleased with
fifty years too late

SURVIVAL / RECOVERY

*When I cannot speak
my sisters will speak for me*
—KIM PAYNE

MONARCH
Beth Goobie

emerging from the cave at the centre of myself.
It has been a locus of meaning for so long—
decades of sitting, face to my firelit core
and watching shadow memories
loom and recede across stone walls.
have i gotten it all yet? have i gotten enough
even to begin to grasp the bigger picture?
this tapestry of inner fire and its shadow partner,
they are necessary each to the other—
one the spark that prevails beyond knowing,
the other the knowing itself; the what, where, when,

sometimes even the why . . . all of these details that explain
the rhythm of one's breathing, its constant narrative
of fear, the way it sculpted a concave identity,
shrinking ever away from surfaces
into the inner trance of the deep.
and that deep, it has spoken to me,
has gathered consensus out of solitude and silence, and proclaimed,

you are more than what was done to you.
take the knowing that now dances face to face with being,
and rise out of your inner cocoon on wings of fire
black-patterned with learned awareness—
a true monarch at peace with the kingdom of self,
and pollinating possibility wherever your heart touches down.

ANNABELLE
Declan Kent

My Belle once wrote that the road
Was iron dark,
That the sky pulsed and shimmered.
She was surprised at the sizzle of her wisdom:
To not love is dangerous.
She thought only of me.
She only thought of me.

Her songs poured out, lustrous, glossy.
She would write of the lips of the lily.
She would write of clean, foamy, green, cresting waves
That are me, who are me,
Swimming to her freckled skin.

She typed her poems on onion-skin paper,
Raised letter cuneiform
And double Xes over a past
She would not let me decipher.

Sometimes she went that way—
Anagramming, veiling,
Layering, leaning away,
Leaving me in ruins
Before building me, home, again.

She didn't have to serve you after closing.
Or, listen to your "Smoke on the Water"
clunky charm.
She could have flung you away faster,
But she quailed,

Could not get a purchase on
Your tight cowboy shirt, its opal snap buttons.
You Tab-learning, Amerika Hick, Huckster, Taker.

If you wanted to bayonet her
With a treacherous message
That she is unsought, unsung,
You did.

If you wanted to be a black sky blade
Severing stars, her spark,
You were.

Sludge seeps through this tragedy house,
Ruining memory and solace.
She harrows her own heart,
Regrets, replays: you did; you were.
You even knew her name.
She stays in, she stays down,
Her eyes dirt, dampened.

But, I am here, too.
I say bite the sweet-peach.
Love-evolve.
Smell the garden-danger flowers.

Day by day, I say lilies, I say sing.
Oh, Anna, Anna, elle, elle,
The bell peal of her name.

Here comes her song.
She breathes out.
Heals the sky.

She is at last the sun coming free,
A rage, brightening, crackling,
That won't save loves new and old,
From the rift she will make in the world.

SURVIVAL / RECOVERY—117

NOVENA 2
Bridget Keating

Tonight, hair-triggered, hungry
and sick like a winter-starved deer,
I ask for your release.

After each sip of straight whiskey,
I clench bits of broken prayers between my teeth,
counting your secrets, your lies, the times you left.

I remember every whispered story,
feel the brush of your tongue on my breasts,
still taste the salt and oil from your skin.

Tonight, I will let my cigarette burn to my fingertips,
burning my flesh raw, hoping later the blisters peel,
removing any trace of you.

ONCE
Judith Krause

She tells them only once.
How it happened and where
and for how long it went on.
She cannot explain
why she didn't say anything before
but she is telling them now
and telling them,
and telling.

DINNER
Heather Bauchop

we still can't sit around a table—the three of us scatter to couches
eating with our plates on our knees

there are days I have to leave the room if Richard eats an apple

how many years was it?
silence, shouting, a sharp report
your chair scraping on the floor
the front door slamming

I ate my dinner in my room

my friend left us a big dining table when she shifted to Perth

I watch the table from across the room

we eat around it sometimes

CALCIUM CARBONATE
Emily MacKinnon

She was a string of pearls: precise,
orderly dependable.

He said he was a jeweller. Said he knew *fresh* water
from salt.

"How 'bout a pearl necklace?" He crowed
Pleased as *punch* with the parallel.

With blunt safety scissors he sawed.

The string frayed.
Fibre by fibre until

snap.

Slowly, slowly she gathered
the scattered beads. Tried to restring them, tried to pretend.

But

They never were
the in
again
right order.

But pearls are still pearls.

Unique;
borne of chafing glass
and rough tides.

Iridescent and
oh, so
Valuable.

ELEMENTS
Ceó Ruaírc

Shall I tell you what I was wearing?

Or shall I say that a *Fire* came
quickly at night
consumed everything I hold dear;
that suffocating smoke surrounded
thick and terrifying;
that today when I think on it my throat
tightens ... I ... struggle to breathe?

Or that the *Water* rose so swiftly
I stood in shock as the gentle river
I thought I knew became
a raging tide, unstoppable;
that I felt small and weak and wondered
if I would survive the disaster;
if I would ever again find
a safe haven inside
my own fragile body?

That now when I see violence
my mind goes someplace else,
not in fire or water, but in the *Air*
like a butterfly, *Nymphalis antiopa*
escaping her cocoon.

But I must also tell you that
I did survive, I did
return to *Earth* grounded
by a strength, a love, a wisdom
unimagined.

And so will you.
And so will you.

ONE
Denise Leduc

Once it was one in four
Now I've heard it is one in three
I wouldn't be surprised if someday soon it becomes one in two
I am the one

Some it damages
Others it destroys
All it scars
I am one of the ones

Once the pain controlled me
I struggled through my existence—the damage...
Numbing myself—first with sex, then alcohol, and finally drugs
Always with drama

Now I am healthy
I fill myself up
With fruit, yoga, fresh air, the company of a dog, and good books
I refuse to give my predators the power to destroy me

Soon—although my scars will always remain I will be healed

This isn't the path I would have chosen
But I will accept this fate
I am strong, fierce, stubborn
They won't break me—not ever
Some they might
So until there is none
I will be a one

TO BELIEVE
Kim Stobbe

My hope for today,
my yearning, my deepest desire is to believe.
To believe in something... someone... someday.
I struggle, I long, I fight just to believe.

I fight to believe that my history need not be a life sentence.
That I am not destined to live out the legacy of ghosts.
That abandonment and fear embedded in a child's heart
need not keep shackled this woman's soul.

I fight to believe that a life exists outside of my mind.
That the echoes of self-loathing can be silenced
to receive a better truth.

I fight to believe that I can break free
from the horrors of past experience.
That neglect and abuse need not anchor me
in a sea of turmoil.
That I can rise from the pit of despair and survive.

I fight to believe that I can be free of nightmares.
That the night can bring peace and solace
not terror and regret.
Just to sleep with the dreams of a child.
Just to sleep.

I fight to believe that I am more than the sum total of my failures;
that this torment is not my destiny;
that healing and forgiveness are possible and
that life can be more than pain and fear.

I fight to believe in the power of my own voice and the journey
that will free me from the bonds of my shadows.
That the answers do lie within me and that they will come
when I am ready.
May I have the strength to receive them.

I fight to believe that there will come a day
when I no longer rage against the demons that haunt my soul.
That in my weakest moments I find my greatest strength.
That someday I will make peace with my ghosts, myself, and my story.
But until I can believe,
I pray for the strength to reach out.
To accept the hands that will pick me up.
To look into the eyes of those who care without judgment or reproach.
To receive pure, unconditional love and support and truly believe
    I deserve it.

And some distant day I will no longer fight to believe;
I will believe
in the wonder of life's possibilities; in the power of my own soul;
    in the strength of connection.
Then I will be free, I will be healed, and I will soar.

UNITE
Kim Payne

I am worthy
I deserve respect
I demand respect
When I cannot speak
My sisters will speak for me
When you try to tear me down
My sisters will work to tear you down
I have a voice
The voice of my sisters
I have the right to be pretty
To put on makeup
Curl my hair
Wear high heels
This is not an invitation
To be disrespected
For you to use me as you wish
I will demand respect
My sisters will demand respect
Our voices will echo
And we will be heard.

ACKNOWLEDGEMENTS

"Birdman," by Byrna Barclay, in *Line Dance: An Anthology of Poetry*, edited by Gerald Hill (Burton House Books, 2016). The poem borrows the lines "the best part of a man / is a woman, her softnesses" from Dave Margoshes's poem "Adam's Rib."

"An Army of Staring Women," by Susie Berg, in *All This Blood* (Piquant Press, 2017).

"Love and Nintendo," by Ruth Daniell, in *The Brightest Thing* (Caitlin Press, 2019).

"monarch," by Beth Goobie, in *breathing at dusk* (Coteau Books, 2017).

"Zipper," by Catherine Graham, was first published in *The Minola Review* and subsequently in her poetry collection *The Celery Forest* (Wolsak & Wynn/Buckrider Books, 2017).

"Honour Killing: A Glosa," by Troni Y. Grande, quotes from Susan Glaspell's *Trifles: A Play in One Act* (Baker's Plays, 1951), 19.

"Black Plums," by Catherine Greenwood, in *The Pearl King and Other Poems* (Brick Books, 2004).

"In the Scheme of Things," by Raye Hendrickson, in *Five Red Sentries* (Thistledown Press, 2019).

"Pulp Non-fiction," by Janis Butler Holm, was first published in *Tessera*, 37–38 (2005): 49, and subsequently in *Women Write Resistance: Poets Resist Gender Violence*, edited by Laura Madeline Wiseman (Hyacinth Girl Press, 2013): 87.

"Woods Wolf Girl," by Cornelia Hoogland, in *Woods Wolf Girl* (Wolsak & Wynn, 2011).

"Five Parts Rape Poem One Part Self-Care," by Kyla Jamieson, first appeared in *Room Magazine* (Volume 40.4) and was also included in *Body Count*, Kyla Jamieson's début poetry collection (Nightwood Editions, 2020). It borrows the phrasing "accidentally say OK" from Morgan Parker's poem "Other People's Comfort Keeps Me Up at Night."

"Once," by Judith Krause, in *Half the Sky* (Coteau Books, 1994).

"LXVIII," by Sonnet L'Abbé, in *Sonnet's Shakespeare* (McClelland and Stewart, 2019).

"Driving Test," by Anne Lévesque, was previously published in *Galleon V* (November 2016)

"Autumn in the East, the Pilot," by Jami Macarty, was previously published as "Autumn in the East" in *The Journal*, 43.3 (Summer 2019). Copyright 2019 by Jami Macarty. Reprinted with permission of Jami Macarty.

"Name Me After a Fish," by Leah MacLean-Evans, was previously published online by the League of Canadian Poets as the winner of the 2018 National Broadsheet Contest.

"The Way the Crocodile Taught Me," by Katrina Naomi, in *The Way the Crocodile Taught Me* (Seren, 2016).

"Sixteen," by Eleonore Schönmaier, in *Wavelengths of Your Song* (MQUP, 2013). Print.

"Wreaths," by Amy Sonoun, was previously published in *Beloit Poetry Journal* (Winter 2014/2015).

RESOURCES FOR SURVIVORS OF ASSAULT

National/Turtle Island
Canadian Resource Centre for Victims of Crime:
    https://crcvc.ca/for-victims/services/
Native Women's Association: https://www.nwac.ca/
Kids Help Phone: https://kidshelpphone.ca/
Pandora's Project: https://pandys.org/

British Columbia
Ending Violence Association of BC:
    http://endingviolence.org/need-help/
British Columbia Society for Male Survivors of Sexual Abuse:
    http://bc-malesurvivors.com/
Vancouver Rape Relief and Women's Shelter:
    http://www.rapereliefshelter.bc.ca/
    24 hour crisis line 1-604-872-8212
Victim Services of BC: https://www2.gov.bc.ca/gov/content/
    justice/criminal-justice/victims-of-crime/victimlinkbc

Alberta
Association of Alberta Sexual Assault Services (AASAS): https://aasas.ca/
Alberta Victim Services: http://victimservicesalberta.com/

Saskatchewan
Hot Peach Pages – International Directory of Domestic Violence Agencies: http://www.hotpeachpages.net/canada/sass.html
Provincial Association of Transition Houses and Services of Saskatchewan: https://pathssk.org/
Sexual Assault Services of Saskatchewan (SASS) – Sexual Assault Services for Men and Women: http://sassk.ca/
Saskatchewan Victim Services: https://www.saskatchewan.ca/residents/justice-crime-and-the-law/victims-of-crime-and-abuse/interpersonal-violence-and-abuse-programs

Manitoba
Klinic Sexual Assault Crisis Program: http://www.klinic.mb.ca/counsel-sexual.htm#
Survivor's Hope Centre: http://survivors-hope.ca/

Ontario
Ontario Coalition of Rape Crisis Centres: https://sexualassaultsupport.ca/
Support Services for Male Survivors of Sexual Abuse: https://www.attorneygeneral.jus.gov.on.ca/english/ovss/male_support_services/
24/7 *Crisis Line:* 1-866-887-0015
Ontario Victim Services: http://www.victimservicesontario.ca/
Victim Support Line: 1-888-579-2888 or (416) 314-2447 in the Toronto area

Quebec
Government of Québec: http://www.agressionssexuelles.gouv.qc.ca/en/resources/index.php
Quebec Victim Services: https://cavac.qc.ca/en/

New Brunswick
Fredericton Sexual Assault Crisis Centre: https://svnb.ca/en/
New Brunswick Victim Services:
https://www2.gnb.ca/content/gnb/en/departments/public-safety/community_safety/content/victim_services.html

Nova Scotia
Avalon Sexual Assault Centre: https://avaloncentre.ca/ & http://avaloncentre.ca/resources/links/
Nova Scotia Victim Services: https://novascotia.ca/just/victim_services/

Prince Edward Island
Prince Edward Island Rape and Sexual Assault Centre: http://www.peirsac.org/links.php
Prince Edward Island Victim Support Services: https://www.princeedwardisland.ca/en/information/justice-and-public-safety/victim-services

Newfoundland and Labrador
Newfoundland and Labrador Sexual Assault Crisis and Prevention Centre: http://nlsacpc.com/
Newfoundland Victim Services: http://www.victimserviceshelp.ca/index.html

Northwest Territories
Hospital-Based 24 hour Crisis Line: http://www.hss.gov.nt.ca/social-services/nwt-help-line (867) 920-2121 or Toll free: 1-800-661-0844
Yellowknife Victim Services: https://www.justice.gov.nt.ca/en/victim-services/ 24-hour Crisis Line (867) 765-8811
Native Women's Association Victim Services: https://www.nativewomensnwt.com/victim-services

Yukon
Yukon Victim Services: http://www.justice.gov.yk.ca/prog/cor/vs/ (867) 993-5831; *After Hours Support VictimLink* 1-800-563-0808

Nunavut
Nunavut Victim Services: https://www.gov.nu.ca/justice/programs-services/victim-services
Nunavut Kamatsiagtut Helpline: Every night from 7-12pm (E/T) Toll Free (867) 979-3333

CONTRIBUTORS

CAROL ALEXANDER's most recent poetry collection is *Environments* (Dos Madres Press). Her poems appear in various anthologies and in journals such as *Aji, The American Journal of Poetry, The Canary, Chiron Review, The Common, Cumberland River Review, Denver Quarterly, Hamilton Stone Review, Pif, One, Poetrybay, Southern Humanities Review, Sweet Tree Review,* terrain.org, *The New Verse News, The Seattle Review of Books,* and *Third Wednesday*. Other work is forthcoming in *Pangyrus* and *Raintown Review*. Alexander's new poetry collection, *Fever and Bone,* will be published in early 2021 by Dos Madres Press.

A CASE Gold Award winner for feature-length creative non-fiction, **ROSEMARY ANDERSON** recently came out about the abuse she endured as a young adult at the hands of a Catholic priest in Kamloops, British Columbia. She launched a civil suit in BC Supreme Court that culminated in fifteen days of trial, believed to be the first time an adult abused by a religious leader has gone through trial in Canada. The judge, to his credit, awarded record-breaking monetary damages against the defendant. Anderson is currently being trued in the unforgiving furnace of writing book-length memoir, a draft of which allowed her to graduate with an MFA from UBC at the youthful age of seventy. In rare but treasured moments, she dares the muse of non-fiction poetry.

ANONYMOUS. "On sleepless nights..." was written near the beginning of what would become the darkest years of the author's life, and it captures the cocktail of emotions that characterized those years. Yet, as painful as it might be for the author to read now, writing poems helped the author process and understand what happened, and in that way, it gave and continues to give him strength.

NATALIE BAKER has been writing since she was a child, but it wasn't until she was a teenager with a penchant for angst, anxiety, and her thesaurus that Baker ventured into poetry. Armed with pen and paper, she spent the summer she was fourteen writing poem after poem in an attempt to unravel a series of events she didn't understand or know how to articulate. Ten years later, she started writing again to begin the process of shedding her guilt and self-blame. Baker would like this new poetry to be part of the conversation that encouraged her to open up about and heal from her trauma—she wants to pay it forward.

Regina writer **BYRNA BARCLAY** is the founder of Burton House Books and has published twelve books of fiction. Beginning with winning the Saskatchewan Culture and Youth First Novel Award for *Summer of the Hungry Pup*, Barclay has won many literary and volunteer awards, culminating in her province's highest honour, the Saskatchewan Order of Merit. Her poetry has appeared in literary magazines such as *Grain* and *Prairie Fire* and in the recent anthology *Line Dance*, edited by Gerald Hill. An advocate for the arts, Barclay has served as president of the Saskatchewan Writers' Guild (twice), the Saskatchewan Book Awards, and the Canadian Mental Health Association in Saskatchewan, and chair of the Saskatchewan Arts Board. Having been a guest lecturer at universities in Canada and the United States, even on board the Oceanic tour to Russia, she is available for workshops, readings, book signings, and visits to book clubs. byrnabarclay@sasktel.net

HEATHER BAUCHOP is a writer, poet, and historian who lives in Dunedin, New Zealand. Her short fiction has appeared in the journals *Headland*, *Alluvia*, and in the 2017 anthology *Fresh Ink* (Cloud Ink Press, Auckland NZ). She is the winner of the 2016 Takahe short story competition. Her poetry has appeared in *Takahe*, *Poetry New Zealand*, and the 2017 and 2020 *Poetry New Zealand Yearbooks*. Her 2018 narrative poetry sequence *The Life in Small Deaths* won the 2018 Kathleen Grattan Prize for a Sequence of Poems. She works in the field of historic heritage.

Beauchop's creative non-fiction has appeared in *Corpus*, a University of Otago blog devoted to the conversation between medicine and the arts.

MARION BECK attended Leeds University, where she earned an Honours degree in Geography and a Graduate Certificate in Education. She was a long-time member of the Saskatchewan Writers' Guild, member and president of the Wascana Writers Group, poetry editor for a number of years for *Green's Magazine*, a member of the Canadian Poetry Association, and an associate member of the League of Canadian Poets. A writer of both non-fiction articles and reviews, she was perhaps best known for her poetry and for a self-published book on autistic children and their families, *The Exorcism of an Albatross*. Her poetry chapbook *Poems for Amazons* opened the exhibition by breast cancer survivors called *Survivors in Search of a Voice* at the MacKenzie Art Gallery in 1996. Beck passed away in June 2020.

SUSIE BERG is a former co-curator of Toronto's Plasticine Poetry reading series and teaches young writers at overnight summer camp. She is the author of two full-length poetry collections, *All This Blood* (2017) and *How to Get Over Yourself* (2014), and three chapbooks. Her work has appeared in journals and anthologies, and she has been a frequent feature on poetry stages. susieberg.ca / @SusieDBerg

ASHLEY-ELIZABETH BEST is a disabled poet and essayist from Kingston, Ontario. Her work can be found in *New Welsh Review*, *CV2*, *Ambit Magazine*, *The Literary Review of Canada*, and *Glasgow Review of Books*, among others. In 2015 she was a finalist for the Robert Kroetsch Award for Innovative Poetry, and her debut collection of poetry, *Slow States of Collapse*, was published with ECW Press. Best's chapbook *Alignment* will be published with Rahila's Ghost Press in spring 2021.

MAROULA BLADES is an Afro-British multifaceted artist living in Berlin. She was nominated for the Amadeu Antonio Prize 2019 for her educational multimedia project "Fringe." She was the first runner-up in the 2018 Tony Quagliano International Poetry Award and and the 2012 winner of the erbacce-prize for poetry. Her works have been published in *The Caribbean Writer*, *Thrice Fiction*, *Harpy Hybrid Review*, *The Freshwater Review*, *Words with Jam*, *Midnight & Indigo*, *Abridged*, *The*

London Reader, Stories of Music Vol. 2, *So It Goes, Newfound Journal,* and by Peepal Tree Press, among others. Regularly, Blades gives bilingual (English and German) poetry workshops in Berlin schools and high schools. Her multimedia projects have been presented at many international literary festivals in Germany. Chapeltown Books (UK) has just released her flash fiction collection *The World in an Eye.*

TARA BORIN is a queer, non-binary settler poet living in traditional Tr'ondëk Hwëch'in territory, Dawson City, Yukon. Their debut full-length collection *The Pit* is out with Nightwood Editions in Spring 2021. taraborinwrites.com.

BEV BRENNA is a Saskatoon poet, novelist, and professor in Curriculum Studies at the University of Saskatchewan. She has published more than a dozen books for young people, including the Wild Orchid trilogy about a teen with autism, which won a Printz Honor Book Award and a Dolly Gray Award, and was shortlisted for a Canadian Governor General's Literary Award. Recent titles include her middle-grade novel *Because of that Crow* (Red Deer Press, 2020) and *The Girl with the Cat* (Red Deer Press, 2019), a picture book set in Saskatoon that resonates with the power of a child's voice and the impact of art.

RONNIE R. BROWN is a writer from Ottawa, Ontario, whose work has appeared in magazines and anthologies in Canada, the United States, and abroad. The author of six collections of poetry, Brown was the winner of the 2006 Acorn-Plantos People's Poetry Award for *States of Matter* (Black Moss Press). In 2013, her long narrative poem *Un-deferred* won the Golden Grassroots Chapbook Contest. Most recently her work has been featured in the anthologies *Tamaracks* (Lummox Press) and *Hearthbeat* (Hidden Brook Press.) In 2020, Brown placed second in the Dr. William Henry Drummond contest for her poem "Because...," about the murder of Pamela George. She is currently working on a collection tentatively entitled *Adventures in Cancerland.*

YANICK CADIEUX is a community counsellor and outreach social worker who works with vulnerable and marginalized people. She works from an anti-oppressive, feminist lens, and this is reflected in her writing. She has been published in various literary and art magazines that challenge mainstream thoughts or processes. *Helen: A literary magazine* published her flash fiction piece "Treasures and Turning Points" and *The Rain, Party, & Disaster Society* online magazine published two of her stories. Cadieux's photography has also been published.

JOAN CRATE is the author of two novels and three books of poetry. In May 2017, her poem "I am a Prophet" was displayed on screen at the U2 concert in Vancouver and Toronto. Her novel *Black Apple* was published in 2016, and along with being shortlisted for the Frank Hegyi Award, it was the recipient of the W.O. Mitchell City of Calgary Award for 2017. Crate currently lives in Calgary, Alberta.

LINDA M. CRATE's works have been published in numerous magazines and anthologies both online and in print. She is the author of seven poetry chapbooks, the latest of which is *the samurai* (Yellow Arrow Publishing, 2020), as well as the novel *Phoenix Tears* (Czykmate Books, 2018). Recently she has published three full-length poetry collections: *Vampire Daughter* (Dark Gatekeeper Gaming, 2020), *The Sweetest Blood* (Cyberwit, 2020), and *Mythology of My Bones* (Cyberwit, 2020).

RUTH DANIELL is a teacher, editor, award-winning writer, and the author of *The Brightest Thing* (Caitlin Press, 2019), a full-length collection of poems about sexual violence, fairy tales, love, and healing. The editor of *Boobs: Women Explore What It Means to Have Breasts* (Caitlin Press, 2016), her work has also appeared in the anthologies *Sustenance: Writers from BC and Beyond on the Subject of Food* (Anvil Press, 2017) and *Watch Your Head: Writers and Artists Respond to the Climate Crisis* (Coach House Press, 2020), and on BC's city buses as part of Poetry in Transit. She holds a Bachelor of Arts (honours) in English literature and writing from the University of Victoria and a Master of Fine Arts in creative writing from the University of British Columbia. She lives in Kelowna, BC, where she is at work on a second collection of poems about birds, climate change, parenthood, fear, and joy.

SAMANTHA FITZPATRICK is a writer and literary publicist based in Newfoundland and Labrador. Her work has appeared in *Paragon* and *Paper Mill Press*. She lives in St. John's.

MYRNA GARANIS is an Alberta-based poet/essayist. Her poems have appeared on Edmonton buses, in magpie, undergarment, pandemic, and hockey literature anthologies. Together with Ivan Sundal, she produced the 2020 Rolling Pins Press anthology *Life of Pie: Prairie Poems and Prose*.

BETH GOOBIE is the author of twenty-five books. Her poem "monarch" originally appeared in her poetry collection *breathing at dusk* (Coteau Books, 2017), which was funded by an SK Arts grant and won two 2018 Saskatchewan Book Awards. "monarch" won the poetry category in the Tisdale Writers Group 2014 writing contest.

SUE GOYETTE lives in K'jipuktuk (Halifax). She has published seven books of poems and a novel. Her latest collection is *Anthesis: a memoir* (Gaspereau Press, 2020). She's been nominated for several awards, including the 2014 Griffin Poetry Prize and the Governor General's Award, and has won the CBC Literary Prize for Poetry, the Earle Birney, the Bliss Carman, the Pat Lowther, the J.M. Abraham Poetry Award, the Relit Award, and the 2015 Lieutenant Governor of Nova Scotia Masterworks Arts Award for her collection *Ocean*. She edited the 2014 Best of Canadian Poetry Anthology, the 2017 Griffin Poetry Prize Anthology, and *Resistance* (University of Regina Press, 2021). Goyette teaches in the Creative Writing Program at Dalhousie University and is the current Poet Laureate of Halifax Regional Municipality.

CATHERINE GRAHAM's sixth poetry collection, *The Celery Forest*, was named a CBC Best Book of the Year and was a finalist for the Fred Cogswell Award for Excellence in Poetry. Her debut novel, *Quarry*, was a finalist for the Sarton Women's Book Award and Fred Kerner Book Award and won an IPPY Award and The Miramichi Reader's Very Best! Book Award. She teaches creative writing at the University of Toronto School of Continuing Studies, where she won an Excellence in Teaching Award. A previous winner of TIFA's Poetry NOW, Graham leads its monthly book club. *Æther: An Out-of-Body Lyric* and her second novel, *The Most Cunning Heart*, are forthcoming. www.catherinegraham.com / @catgrahampoet

TRONI Y. GRANDE teaches Shakespeare, drama, and feminist theory in the English Department at the University of Regina. She studies "she-tragedy"—a kind of tragedy focusing on the woman as a suffering, beautiful victim of patriarchy. Her creative writing publications include several poems, and a memoir excerpt in the 2016 Demeter Press anthology *Borderlands and Crossroads: Writing the Motherland* (edited by Jane Satterfield and Laurie Kruk). Her work-in-progress is *Baba's Pyrogies*, a memoir about the legacy of her maternal grandmother, a Ukrainian settler in east-central Alberta.

CATHERINE GREENWOOD has held a variety of jobs—from working in a community services thrift store to teaching literary theory in a Chinese university. Her first book, *The Pearl King and Other Poems*, based upon the life of the inventor of the cultured pearl, was a Kiriyama Prize Notable Book. Her second collection, *The Lost Letters*, centers on a sequence inspired by the story of Heloise and Abelard. Greenwood is currently a PhD researcher at the University of Sheffield, where she's pursuing an interest in Gothic poetry.

LORI HANSON is a scholar-activist who advocates and practises feminist, action-oriented research and education on health-related issues. She is a professor in the Department of Community Health and Epidemiology at the University of Saskatchewan. Her most recent co-edited book, *Much Madness, Divinest Sense: Women's Stories of Mental Health and Health Care*, was inspired by rage, hope, and a poem.

GILLIAN HARDING-RUSSELL has five poetry collections published, most recently *Uninterrupted* (Ekstasis Editions, 2020), and a short chapbook *Megrim* (The Alfred Gustav Press, 2021) to be released in the spring. Her previous collection *In Another Air* (Radiant Press, 2018) was shortlisted for the Saskatchewan Book Awards City of Regina Award. Her poems have been shortlisted three times for *Exile's* Gwendolyn MacEwen chapbook competition, and in 2016 won first place for the sequence *Making Sense*.

Working as a massage therapist allows **RAYE HENDRICKSON** to inhabit the inner workings of our bodies, and her poetry explores the intricacies of relationships, the mysteries and curiosities of science and nature, and the challenges of our mind and spirit. Celebrating her home terrain of Saskatchewan, Hendrickson says the prairies allow her to breathe and feel a genuine sense of place. Her work has been published in *Spring*,

The Society, *Event*, and the anthology *line dance*. Her first book of poetry, *Five Red Sentries*, was shortlisted for two 2020 Saskatchewan Book Awards.

DEE HOBSBAWN-SMITH's award-winning poetry, essays, fiction, and journalism have appeared in literary journals, newspapers, websites, magazines, and anthologies in Canada, the United States, and elsewhere. She is the author of seven books and one poetry chapbook. Her eighth book, an essay collection titled *Bread & Water*, will be published by University of Regina Press in 2021. A retired Red Seal chef, she holds an MFA in Writing and is currently completing her MA in Literature. She lives west of Saskatoon, Saskatchewan, is married, and has two sons.

JANIS BUTLER HOLM has served as Associate Editor for *Wide Angle*, the film journal. Her prose, poems, and performance pieces have appeared in small-press, national, and international magazines. Her plays have been produced in the United States, Canada, and the United Kingdom.

JESSE HOLTH is a writer, editor, and poet living on Lekwungen and W̱SÁNEĆ territory. Her poems have appeared in *Room*, *Grain*, *CV2*, *Prairie Schooner*, and other publications. She previously served as editor-in-residence for The Puritan's *Town Crier*, guest editor for *antilang.*, and assistant poetry editor for *The Tishman Review*. She is currently working on two full-length collections.

CORNELIA HOOGLAND's recent publications are *Dressed in Only a Cardigan, She Picks Up Her Tracks in the Snow* (Baseline Press, 2021); and *Cosmic Bowling* (Guernica, 2020), a collaboration with the visual artist Ted Goodden. *Trailer Park Elegy* and *Woods Wolf Girl* were finalists for national awards. Hoogland's expertise in Red Riding Hood includes publication of a PhD thesis on the fairy tale, articles, plays, fiction, and her book *Woods Wolf Girl*. Red Riding Hood as a prototype of the missing and murdered female is her ongoing concern. Hoogland was the 2019 writer-in-residence for the Al Purdy A-Frame and the Whistler Festival. She lives and writes on unceded Puntledge and K'omox territories on Hornby Island in the Salish Sea.
http://www.corneliahoogland.com/

LOUISA HOWEROW's poems have appeared in a number of anthologies, among them *I Found It at the Movies: An Anthology of Film Poems* (Guernica), *Gush: Menstrual Manifestos for Our Times* (Frontenac House), and *Another Dysfunctional Cancer Poem Anthology* (Mansfield Press). Her poem "Why Scrabble" was selected for Poem in Your Pocket, 2020.

TARYN HUBBARD's writing has appeared in journals and anthologies across Canada such as *CV2, subTerrain, Canadian Literature, Room, The Capilano Review, Canadian Woman Studies, filling Station, Lemon Hound, Boobs: Women Explore What It Means to Have Breasts* (Caitlin Press), and many others. She currently lives and writes in Maple Ridge, British Columbia, as their Port Haney artist-in-residence with her partner Aaron Moran. Her first poetry collection, *Desire Path*, debuted with Talonbooks in September 2020. tarynhubbard.com

After struggling with music, **KEITH INMAN** began writing to deal with the rhythms in his head. His teacher, an American war resister who had studied at U of T during the tail end of the Frye/McLuhan era, eventually suggested poetry, to "get that flowery shit" out of his work. She loved holding class in museums, where she'd talk about Impressionism and working-class life in landscape. "You should write like that in your blue-collar style," she said, pointing at peasants gleaning fields in a mountain's shadow. Inman has six books of poetry. His latest are *The War Poems: Screaming at Heaven, SEAsia* (pronounced Seize-ya), and *The Way History Dries*, all from Black Moss Press.

KYLA JAMIESON lives and relies on the unceded traditional territories of the Musqueam, Squamish, and Tsleil-Waututh Nations. Her début poetry collection, *Body Count*, contains poems written both before and after the disabling concussion she experienced at age twenty-six, and was released by Nightwood Editions in Spring 2020. Find her on a rock next to a river or at kylajamieson.com.

JO JEFFERSON (they/them) is a Toronto-based queer writer, parent, and community worker who grew up in Nova Scotia. Their poetry, short fiction, and personal essays have been published by *Prairie Fire, The Antigonish Review, Understorey Magazine, Syracuse Cultural Workers*, and in various anthologies. When they're not writing or reading, Jefferson hangs out with their kids, works with queer elders at a community centre, plays softball, explores the world, and facilitates workshops with curious creators of all ages.

POLLY JOHNSON (pseudonym) is a writer with one published novel and whose poetry has been accepted by a couple of well-known publications. She has worked in education most of her life but has recently stopped work to tutor privately while she works on her latest novel.

ELIZABETH JOHNSTON is a gender studies scholar, creative writer, professor, and mother of two daughters. She is a founding member of the four-woman writer's group, Straw Mat Writers, a former advisory board member of Take Back the News, and a facilitator for writing-as-healing workshops for survivors of sexual assault and breast cancer. She also teaches English at Monroe Community College and courses in Women and Gender Studies at The College at Brockport in Rochester, New York. Johnston's writing appears in many journals and edited collections and has been nominated for three Pushcart prizes and a Best of the Net award. Her writing that deals explicitly with the subject of sexual assault appears in *The Atlantic*, *New Verse News*, *Tuck Magazine*, *Rogue Agent*, *Room*, and in the collection *Veils, Halos, and Shackles*. http://strawmatwriters.weebly.com

MARIANNE JONES's work has appeared in *Wascana Review*, *Room*, *Danforth Review*, and several anthologies, including *All We Can Hold* (Sage Hill Press), *Writing Menopause* (Inanna Publications), and *Indra's Net* (Bennison Books). Her poetry has won awards from The Canadian Authors Association, Northwestern Ontario Writers Workshop, The Word Guild, *Writers Digest*, and the Poetry Matters Project. Her novel *Maud and Me* has been slated for publication by Crossfield Publishing in 2021. Jones lives in Thunder Bay with her husband Reg.

LUCIE KAVANAGH lives in the west of Ireland and worked with adults with disabilities for twenty years. She had to stop for health reasons but is now building a new life working with animals. Lucie blogs about mental health (http://square1one.blogspot.ie/) and volunteers for an organization that works to dispel stigma around mental illness. She also writes poetry and stories. Kavanagh loves reading, art, and looking after her two dogs, four cats, five chickens, and usually a foster pet or two!

BRIDGET KEATING holds a PhD in Mexican history and visual culture and has taught at the University of Regina since 2008. Her work has been published in national and international anthologies and journals and *Red Ceiling*, her first book of poetry, was nominated for numerous awards.

KEIR (pseudonym). The poem is dedicated to family members and other supporters of survivors of sexual assault. The "claiming" in the poem is made easier by the fact that the person in the poem returned home to apologize to his victim, shortly before his death.

Poet, performer, and playwright **PENN KEMP** has been celebrated as a trailblazer since her first publication of poetry by Coach House (1972). She was London's inaugural Poet Laureate (2010–13) and Western University's Writer-in-Residence (2009–10). Chosen as the League of Canadian Poets' Spoken Word Artist (2015), Kemp has long been a keen participant/activist in Canada's cultural life. Recent titles include *Fox Haunts, Local Heroes, Barbaric Cultural Practice*, and *Jack Layton: Art in Action* (ed.).

"**DECLAN KENT**" is a poetic persona of Deirdre Maultsaid (she/her). Maultsaid has had poetry and creative non-fiction published in literary journals and anthologies, including *3Elements Literary Review, Canthius, CV2*, the book *Double Lives* (McGill-Queens University Press), *Filling Station, Grain, The Lavender Review, Pif, Prairie Fire, The Puritan, Riddle Fence, untethered, White Wall Review,* and many others. She is a queer white writer living in Burnaby, British Columbia, on the unceded territory of the Coast Salish Peoples. She teaches Communications at Kwantlen Polytechnic University. It is well-known that Deirdre Maultsaid is a restored, whole person who has survived bullying and sexual assaults. @deirdmaultsaid / https://deirdremaultsaid.com/

SHANNON KERNAGHAN writes and creates visual art from Alberta, Canada. She enjoyed life as a "digital nomad" for many years, travelling and writing from her RV even before the cool term was created. Her work appears in books, magazines, and journals—poetry, fiction, and everything between—and she continues to tell her stories at www.ShannonKernaghan.com.

JUDITH KRAUSE calls Saskatchewan home. She is a longtime member of the provincial writing community and proudly served a two-year term as the fifth Saskatchewan Poet Laureate. Recent publications include poems in *Grain* 42.2 and 46.1 and in the anthology *Heartwood* (2018). Author of five poetry books and a collaborative chapbook, Krause is working on a sixth poetry collection.

SONNET L'ABBÉ is the author of three collections of poetry, *A Strange Relief*, *Killarnoe*, and *Sonnet's Shakespeare*, as well as the chapbook *Anima Canadensis*. In 2000, they won the Bronwen Wallace Memorial Award for most promising writer under 35, and in 2014, they were the guest editor of Best Canadian Poetry in English. L'Abbé lives on Vancouver Island and is a professor of creative writing at Vancouver Island University.

ELLIE ROSE LANGSTON is a university student from London, England, and is currently residing in Halifax while pursuing her bachelor's degree in medical sciences. Growing up, she was an avid reader and started to write during her early teenage years. After taking a long break from writing, the idea for "When you looked at me did you see me?" came to her overnight. Writing the poem helped her deal with the traumatic aftermath of campus sexual assault. She is now a proud survivor and advocate for the prevention of campus sexual violence. This will be her first published work.

Saskatoon writer **KATHERINE LAWRENCE** is the author of four poetry collections, including *Never Mind* (winner of the John V. Hicks Long Manuscript Award and nominated for Book of the Year, Saskatchewan). Her young adult novel-in-verse *Stay* won the North American Moonbeam Award for children's poetry. A new collection of poems is forthcoming (Turnstone Press). Other titles include *Lying to Our Mother* and *Ring Finger, Left Hand* (both from Coteau Books). Honours include Best First Book, the City of Regina Writing Award, the gritLit Award, and two nominations for the Anne Szumigalski Poetry Award. Her work has been longlisted twice for the CBC Poetry Award.

Lawrence's work has appeared in *Best Canadian Poetry*, CBC Books, *The Windsor Review*, *Prairie Fire*, *Hamilton Arts & Letters*, *CV2*, and *Grain*, among others. She holds an MFA in Writing from the University of Saskatchewan and is a former writer-in-residence with the Saskatoon Public Library.

DENISE LEDUC is a writer currently living in small-town Saskatchewan. She balances her time between writing and running a yoga and fitness studio. Leduc currently writes for the *Davidson Leader*. Her works have also been published on the labour news website *Rank and File*, the homeschooling magazine *Life Learning*, as well as the news website *Rabble*. Leduc founded the charity Prairie Bear Books, which works to promote literacy and get books into the homes of at-risk children and youth. She currently serves as the board's president.

EMMA LEE's publications include *The Significance of a Dress* (Arachne, 2020) and *Ghosts in the Desert* (IDP, 2015). She co-edited *Over Land, Over Sea* (Five Leaves, 2015), is Review Editor for *The Blue Nib Literary Magazine*, and reviews for magazines and blogs at http://emmalee1.wordpress.com.

MARSHALL L. wrote "Yes, Those Were Crimes of Violence" as an act of grace while stumbling to put his shoes on and head out the door to work. "It was unrelenting as it streamed into my consciousness in fragmented pieces... I should hardly think I wrote it and yet I did, as I was the victim in subject of said violence. The Criminal Injuries Compensation Board had just vindicated me of my hateful and abusive past with their words and a substantial financial award. I was to be free of a personal history that kept me in bondage, and this poem was its culmination." The conception of this poem marked the beginning of his writing, and he has since completed the first draft of a memoir alongside a personal book of poetry. Lee hopes to continue writing and continue his journey to inner freedom.

KRISTIE BETTS LETTER is the author of *Fire in the Hole* (Engine Books, 2019) and *Under-Worldly* (Editorial L'Aleph, 2015). She's published pieces in *The Massachusetts Review*, *Washington Square*, *The North Dakota Quarterly*, *The Southern Humanities Review*, and *Consequence*, among others, with work upcoming in *Waves: Women Writing on Virginia Woolf*. When not writing, she teaches Innovation and Design Thinking in Colorado. She's earned four NEH fellowships, the Boulder Valley Impact Award for teaching, and the national Conrad Innovative Teacher of the Year Award. kristiebettsletter.com

ANNE LÉVESQUE's poetry, short fiction, and essays have appeared in Canadian and international journals. Her début novel *Lucy Cloud* was published in 2018. She lives on the west coast of Cape Breton Island, Nova Scotia.

HALLI LILBURN lives in Lethbridge, Alberta. She has works published with Edge Science Fiction and Fantasy, Leap Books, *Carte Blanche*, *Poetry Quarterly*, and many other publications. She is an artist, librarian, and creative writing instructor. hallililburn.blogspot.com

JAMI MACARTY is the author of *The Minuses* (Center for Literary Publishing, 2020), winner of the 2020 New Mexico-Arizona Book Award for Poetry Arizona. She is also the author of three chapbooks, including *Mind of Spring* (Vallum Chapbook Series, 2017), winner of the 2017 Vallum Chapbook Award. As a teacher at Simon Fraser University and an editor at *The Maynard*, she supports the creative works of other writers. Her writing has been supported by Arizona Commission on the Arts and British Columbia Arts Council, and by editors of literary journals such as *Arc Poetry Magazine*, *Beloit Poetry Journal*, and *The Capilano Review*. http://www.jamimacarty.com

LAURIE MACKIE is a graduate of Kwantlen Polytechnic University's Bachelor of Arts Creative Writing program and is nearing completion of her Bachelor of Fine Arts degree. A two-time alumnus of Sage Hill's Writers' Retreat, she has recently completed her debut fiction manuscript, *Crossing to Jordan*. Her interests lie in fiction, creative non-fiction, and poetry. Mackie has plans to pursue her master's degree and to complete her first non-fiction manuscript, *Letters to Jeannie*. Publications include *Pearls*, *After the Pause*, *Misfit Lit*, *The Black Napkin*, *Pulp*, the Marjorie McIntosh contest, and *untethered*.

EMILY MACKINNON is an editor with Nimbus Publishing in Halifax, Nova Scotia. She is a journalism graduate of the University of King's College, a new mom, and occasional writer.

LEAH MACLEAN-EVANS writes poems and stories in Ottawa. Her work has appeared in *CV2*, *untethered*, *Qwerty*, *On Spec Magazine*, *The Globe and Mail*, and elsewhere. Most recently, she won Arc's 2020 Poem of the Year Contest. She was also the 2017 fiction winner of the Blodwyn Memorial Prize. She has an MFA in Writing from the University of Saskatchewan, is the proofreader of *Grain*, and a director of *Canthius*. "Name Me After a Fish" is a reflection on navigating our patriarchal society as a woman who experienced CSA, and won the League of Canadian Poets' National Broadsheet Contest in 2018. @PenAndDragon / www.macleanevans.ca

KIM MANNIX is a poet, fiction writer, and journalist currently residing on Treaty 6 territory in Sherwood Park, Alberta. She has been published in several journals and anthologies in Canada and the United States and is a contributing editor of *Watch Your Head*, a climate crisis anthology. You can find her on Twitter @KimMannix, usually posting about kids, cats, and music.

AMBER MOORE is a SSHRC-funded PhD candidate and Killam Laureate at the University of British Columbia, studying language and literacy education with the Faculty of Education. Her research interests include adolescent literacy, feminist pedagogies, teacher education, and trauma literature, particularly YA sexual assault narratives. Moore also enjoys writing poetry and creative non-fiction.

Born in Montreal, **DANA MORENSTEIN** is a poet of both Jewish and Mexican descent. As a young child, she moved to Saskatchewan, where she still resides. After graduating from the University of Regina with her Bachelor of Education degree, she taught for three years. During her third year of teaching, Morenstein realized that to create change, she would need to do so outside of the system which resisted it so much. She now lives happily on the fringes of society.

CONTRIBUTORS—151

MARION MUTALA has a master's degree in educational administration and taught for thirty years. With a passion for the arts, she loves to write, sing, and play guitar, travel and read. Marion is the author of fifteen books, including the bestselling and award-winning children's books *Baba's Babushka: A Magical Ukrainian Christmas* (Anna Pidrucheny Award, 2010), *Baba's Babushka: A Magical Ukrainian Easter* (shortlisted for a Saskatchewan Book Award, 2013), and *Baba's Babushka: A Magical Ukrainian Wedding* (The High Plains Children's Book Award, 2015), and *Kohkum's Babushka: A Magical Metis/Ukrainian Tale*. Her debut poetry collection *Ukrainian Daughter's Dance* was published in 2016. Mutala recently released a chapbook called *Earth Angels: Operation Angel* and *Baba's Babushka: A Magical Journey to Ukraine*, included in a 10th Anniversary edition of her collection called *Baba's Babushka: Magical Ukrainian Adventures* (2020). www.babasbabushka.com

KATRINA NAOMI's third collection, *Wild Persistence*, was published by Seren in 2020 and was awarded an Authors' Foundation Award by the UK Society of Authors. Her poetry has appeared on the London Underground and in *The TLS*, *The Spectator*, *The Poetry Review*, and *Modern Poetry in Translation*, as well as on BBC Radio and TV. Her second collection, *The Way the Crocodile Taught Me*, was published by Seren (2016). Other publications include *Typhoon Etiquette* (Verve Poetry Press, 2019), *Hooligans* (Rack Press), *The Girl with the Cactus Handshake* (Templar Poetry), which was shortlisted for the London New Writers Award and received an Arts Council England award, *Charlotte Brontë's Corset* (Brontë Society), and *Lunch at the Elephant and Castle* (Templar Poetry), which won the Templar Poetry Pamphlet Competition. Naomi holds a PhD in creative writing from Goldsmiths, University of London, where she is an honorary postdoctoral researcher. She lives in Cornwall (UK). http://www.katrinanaomi.co.uk/

MARINA NEMAT was born in 1965 in Tehran, Iran. After the Islamic Revolution of 1979, she was arrested at the age of sixteen and spent more than two years in Evin, a political prison in Tehran, where she was tortured and came very close to execution. She came to Canada in 1991 and has called it home ever since. Her memoir *Prisoner of Tehran*

(Penguin Canada) was published in 2007, and she wrote her second book, *After Tehran: A Life Reclaimed* (2010), while she was an Aurea Fellow at University of Toronto's Massey College. She has served on the board of directors at the Canadian Centre for Victims of Torture, Vigdis (a Norwegian charitable organization that provides assistance to female political prisoners around the world), Writers in Exile at PEN Canada, and the International Council of the Human Rights Foundation in the United States. Nemat teaches memoir writing at the School of Continuing Studies at University of Toronto.

KELLY NICKIE is an avid reader, writer, and coffee drinker living within the perimeter highway of Winnipeg, Manitoba. She enjoys finding mundane objects and phrases of the everyday and turning them into second thoughts. Her work has been published in *iō Literary Journal*, *The Broken Spine*, *Juice*, *Generation*, *Door = Jar*, *Synaeresis*, *The Curious Element*, and in the *Winnipeg Free Press*.

DONNA J.A. OLSON has an imaginative and somewhat strange mind. She enjoys writing things that mean something and that she can make the emotions come across. She is a young author who lives in Northern Alberta with her family and many animals. With a love for a variety of things, as a teenager she found her voice in writing and deciding to pursue it. She writes not because it is easy, but she has something to say in so many different ways. From articles, to short stories, novels, and poetry, Olson creates lives and shows every emotion that goes along with them.

KIM PAYNE is a mother and poet who loves the colour red and a rich mocha. She believes you are never too old to dream and practises this herself. Her work has been most recently published in *Vaughan Street Doubles* and *Nightingale & Sparrow* literary magazines.

HEATHER READ works in publishing. She is a singer/songwriter and band member of Peach & Quiet, the Wayward Sirens, and formerly of Clancy's Front Porch. She ran a songwriters circle in Victoria, British Columbia, and lives on a Gulf Island in the Salish Sea. She has been writing poems and songs since she was seven. This is her first published work.

BRUCE RICE is the Saskatchewan Poet Laureate (2019–2021), an essayist, and editor. His six collections of poetry include *The Vivian Poems* (Radiant Press, 2020), on the life of street photographer Vivian Maier. Rice was a professional acquaintance of the father in the poem, a respected social scientist whose life course could not be more opposite to that of his son.

CEÓ RUAÍRC writes from wild places, inspired by the wonder of the natural world.

ELEONORE SCHÖNMAIER's new collection *Field Guide to the Lost Flower of Crete* is forthcoming in 2021 from McGill-Queen's University Press. *Wavelengths of Your Song* (MQUP, 2013) was published in German translation in 2020 by parasitenpresse (Cologne). Schönmaier, a former nurse, is also the author of *Dust Blown Side of the Journey* (MQUP, 2017) and *Treading Fast Rivers* (MQUP). Greek, Dutch, Scottish, American, and Canadian composers have set her poems to music. She has won the Alfred G. Bailey Prize, the Earle Birney Prize, the Sheldon Currie Fiction Prize (second place), and the 2019 National Broadsheet Contest. Her poetry has been included in the League of Canadian Poets and the Academy of American Poets' Poem in Your Pocket Day brochure, and has been widely anthologized, including in *Best Canadian Poetry*. Born and raised in a remote settlement in the northern Canadian wilderness, Schönmaier now divides her time between Atlantic Canada and coastal Europe. eleonoreschonmaier.com

AMY SONOUN is a pseudonym.

KIM STOBBE is the director of both a Canadian and a Peruvian NGO. To the world, looking in, she had a dream life: a wonderful husband, beautiful children, incredible friends, and a successful career. But inside she was imploding. After decades of hiding behind masks, denying her secrets, and negating memories, she could no longer ignore the effects of her childhood sexual abuse. The eating disorder, flashbacks, night terrors, body memories, and anxiety were chipping away at the facade she had fought so long to maintain. If not for her therapists, husband, children, and friends, she would not be here today. The "family" that surrounds her now bless her life with the love, support, kindness, laughter, and joy she never thought possible. Stobbe's mission has become transforming "pain to purpose," a phrase she has tattooed on her arm. She now believes in a life of endless possibilities.

JILL M. TALBOT attended Simon Fraser University for psychology before pursing her passion for writing. Her work has appeared in *Geist, Rattle, Poetry Is Dead, The Puritan, Matrix, subTerrain, The Tishman Review, The Cardiff Review,* and PRISM. She won the PRISM Grouse Grind Lit Prize and third place for the Geist Short Long-Distance Contest, and she was shortlisted for the Matrix Lit POP Award for fiction and the Malahat Far Horizons Award for poetry. Talbot lives in Vancouver, British Columbia.

DANIELLE WONG is the author of *Bubble Fusion*, a collection of poems about raising a child with autism. Her other work has appeared in *Montreal Writes, Soft Cartel, Tipton Poetry, The Daily Drunk, Kalopsia Lit, Pendemic,* and *The Pine Cone Review*. Her work has also been found in various anthologies, including *Patterns, Lean In, Overture,* and *The Warbler's Song*. Her work is forthcoming in *Chronicling the Days* in spring 2021 from Guernica Editions. She enjoys attending poetry marathons, walking in forests, listening to crickets, and hanging out with her family. http://www.daniellewong.ca

Inspiring others to try "writing the self" as complementary medicine, **SUZANNE WOOD** believes in the magic of her word balm poems and narratives to soothe her symptoms as she copes with multiple autoimmune connective tissue diseases. Her writing has been published in anthologies and periodicals, in addition to being displayed publicly at "InSight 2," a juried international health humanities public symposium, and on the "Poetry Walk" at the University of Alberta hospital. Wood is a writer, poet, blogger, and patient advocate who enjoys tossing out words recklessly and playfully on her blog: www.wantonwordflirt.com.

ED WOODS was born in Toronto and now lives in Dundas, Ontario. Through attending poetry workshops, established writers gave great encouragement to expand upon life experiences, and a casual interest in poetry became a passion. His heartfelt interest in Industrial Poetry developed from experiences of employment and observations in the field of sciences and infrastructure. His first poem, "Pipelines," was published in 2003 and was related to work as a crew member upon Alberta natural gas lines. Topics to follow related to being recreation instructor, aircraft pilot, chemical tanker driver, telephone cable splicer, night shift taxi driver, and lately, as a municipal snowplow operator. Woods has several self-published chapbooks of poetry and short stories.